Thought Shifting

"How To Remove The Negative Inner Voice in 30 Days"

RICK SARUNA

Forward by
Paris Saruna, M.A.

i

Dedication

I dedicate this book to my wife Patti, my two amazing children, Paris and Ricky, and my Mom.

I could never have done any of this without the lessons of life you have all taught me.

People often say their soul mate is someone who is so similar and shares such common ground. Well, I think my soul mate is the woman that questions me and pushes me to new levels. She makes me consider so many things regarding how to make life more enjoyable and better in every way. For that, Patti, I cannot thank you enough. All I can do is love you and appreciate you more than you'll ever know.

To Paris, my daughter and always my little girl. You have taught me how to live, love, and enjoy life. You make me proud and taught me what love is all about. It also makes me proud that you've gone into a similar field and have a desire to help others. Your love of travel and experiencing new things reminds me of my own passions, which began around the same time in my life. I love you and thank you for being you. One could only wish to have such an amazing daughter. I look forward to you helping us share these processes with the world.

My son, Ricky. What can you say about your namesake? You have taught me how to stay young and to persevere. You have also shown me that happiness is more important than anything. Life is about living and having fun and we must never forget that. I am so proud of you and the accomplishments you've achieved so far in life. The future belongs to you and your dreams and desires. I look forward to creating many more goals and dreams with you. Your thoughts, insights, and passions have inspired me in ways you would never know. I love you and I thank you for being you.

To my Mom. You have always been there, no matter what. You have (and still do!) always support me in so many ways, that just knowing you're there makes me feel stronger and safer. Your love, encouragement, and lessons in life have allowed me to become the person I am today. I love you and thank you.

To My Dad, he may not be here in body, but is in spirit. He knows I know he is proud.

To Lucky and Layla. You never leave our sides and it's amazing to feel your unconditional love. Every day is a great day to these two! Never a complaint, never an off day. Always happy to see us and to be in our presence. So much to learn from two soulful, heart-warming puppies that will always remain so close to our hearts.

To my wonderful and amazing clients. You are all the best and I'm so thankful to have met each and every one of you on this amazing path in our lives. I've been gifted to have been able to help you in your journey that has become my own.

To all of you reading this. I thank you for your support and I hope to meet many of you in seminars, classes, or in our clinic.

A Special Thanks and Mention

To my friend and author John Schlarbaum who was amazing at assisting me with the organization of this work and helping it come alive. Thanks John for your assistance, your kindness and your friendship.

Forward
By Paris Saruna, M.A.

While studying educational psychology in graduate school, I learned a lot about individual development and learning. We have all been children and have one major similarity: we have been taught everything we know. All of our experiences are teachings, whether they were intended or not. School is another teaching that's completely structured with intended lessons. It's supposed to prepare us for life, right?

In educational psychology, we study child development within the context of school. School is a huge point of reference for many experiences, as this is where children continuously learn. What I found so incredibly surprising was that students were not taught one of the most important life lessons: how to think positively. Students are taught how to add and subtract, how to dribble a basketball, and how to cooperate with others. All lessons are based on development for improvement that is cognitive, physical, or social. There are NO emotional development lessons taught to students. One's emotional well-being includes aspects of self-esteem, life satisfaction, happiness, optimism, anxiety, depression, and the management and coping of these emotions.

I hope to one day make an educational change to incorporate emotional wellness classes into school curriculums. I have learned that it is crucial for individuals to be taught thought management. Children need to learn exactly how to worry less and enjoy life more, which will lead to happier adults. Since childhood, we have been allowing stress to affect our levels of success, whether in school, at work, or with personal matters.

So, guess what? You have gone through your entire life without having one proper lesson on emotional well-being. Emotional wellness is often referred to as the optimal state of being. Yes, this means being happy, optimistic, and free of stress. Why on earth has this lesson been skipped from the teachings of life?

Well this is about to change! The material that you will find in Thought Shifting is your key to health and happiness. Happiness is a choice and a decision; reading Thought Shifting is the best action of choice because it will teach you things that will help you quickly and easily.

If you ask me, it makes a lot more sense that happy people would be more successful than unhappy people, which they are. It is also refreshing to know that happy people have the ability to attract other happy, optimistic people. Ever hear of the saying that says you will be like the five people you spend the most time with? Think about that for a minute. The saying is trying to explain that you will actually take on characteristics of those you surround yourself with. Do you surround yourself with happy and optimistic people?

Thought Shifting will not only explain why you should change your thinking, but actually how to do it! The techniques in this book make more sense than anything you have ever experienced or tried because it works! It will work for you too, as long as you apply these simple, new processes.

Take this material from Thought Shifting and read it twice. Take it, practice it, and teach it to your children and loved ones. Let us help and change the world, one person at a time and one thought at a time. Together, we can all live a happier and more fulfilling life. I leave you with my favourite quote from the book:

"You cannot quickly change the world, but you can quickly change your world by changing your thoughts."
- Rick Saruna

"*Your worst enemy cannot harm you as much as your own unguarded thoughts.*"
Buddha

Thought Shifting

"How To Remove The Negative Inner Voice in 30 Days"

*"There is little difference in people,
but that little difference makes a big difference.
The little difference is attitude.
The big difference is whether it is positive
or negative."*
W. Clement Stone

Chapter One

Thought Shifting

How To Remove The Negative Inner Voice In 30 Days

If you asked any parent what they wished for their children, they would say, "Happiness." This simple hope for a child is something most of us chase throughout our lives. What is life without happiness? What is life without joy? An aspiration so simple, yet a process that seems so complicated.

Imagine if one could harness the art of happiness and joy and pass it onto their children, their families and friends.

The quality of life is dependent on the quality of a person's thoughts and their thinking. A person can't have negative thoughts and be happy. It's not possible. Conversely, a happy person can't be so with negative thinking. The two are polar opposites. In order to achieve and maintain a level of happiness, one must remove the negative inner voice and replace it with thoughts of joy and happiness. It sounds so simple. It sounds so easy! For many, it's like chasing the elusive white rabbit in the snow. It's a desire filled with good intention but short on success.

After working with thousands of clients as a Clinical Therapist and the Director of Body & Mind in Windsor, Ontario, I recognized the difficulties experienced by those attending my clinic. It seemed that no matter what the issue, there was one underlying similarity: all these people suffered from a case of negativity, brought on by someone or something in the past. Add in a negative event with a level of intensity and it becomes a recipe for a life of frustrations and ongoing difficulties.

With conventional therapies and processes, the immediate idea is to remove the negative issue or event and suddenly you'll become happy again. Another great theory on paper that falls short in real life. Friends and family will tell you to be happy and positive but it just isn't that easy. If it were, everyone would be doing it.

After interviewing and implementing various systems, methods, and techniques, I discovered some startling similarities that could be changed, released, and removed. This occurred with regular and consistent results client after client. Happiness improved, including attitudes and quality of life. The key was not only focusing on the issue or the trauma, which was only part of the solution. The other part was to teach a person to start to think differently.

This became a step-by-step process, breaking down what to do and how to do it. It had to be something that everyone could do and do it automatically.

Thought Shifting was born many years ago and is used daily to help keep and maintain the changes in those people experiencing a negative inner voice. Thought Shifting is also used in conjunction with removing issues experienced by these individuals. These issues are what bring people in. Thought Shifting keeps them out!

By learning and implementing the processes of Thought Shifting, you will create change at a deep level; perhaps for most of you, for the first time gain control of your inner voice and your life.

Thought Shifting will quickly work on the most important part of your change: your thoughts and your thinking. Change your thoughts, change your thinking, and change your life forever!

Introduction and Background Information

Many years ago, before I was officially in the "stress reduction" field, I owned some retail stores that I started up right out of university. I was considered more than successful, making money from Day One and soon had several locations with quite a few employees. It wasn't long before we were doing half a million dollars in business with an idea I'd cultivated from scratch in the 1980's. What began as a hobby became larger and larger, growing into something that took me in a direction I wasn't sure I wanted to be in forever. I had an extensive background in psych, human behaviour, and development, all fields I originally thought I'd pursue as a career. However, the higher education experience of university didn't shed light in a way that encouraged me to look forward to such a lifelong profession. Instead, after completing my studies, I felt discouraged and disillusioned. I questioned the whole field. Worse than that, I began to question myself. I realized the more I knew, the more I didn't know! It was not a nice feeling. The materials I'd spent four years learning didn't work in a way I wanted, expected, or hoped they would.

I went to an excellent private school in Minnesota. They were very good at identifying problems and then handing out labels, but where were the solutions to all the problems that seemed so easy to label? Where were the answers? Why didn't this stuff work? If it did, why would people have the problems that so many have and suffer with each day? I was helping people more when not applying those learned methods, all the while looking for new solutions.

Many psychological studies are the most memorable of my school years. Some were fascinating, educational, and a few funnier than heck. Take the study by a group of students who voluntarily had themselves committed to a psych ward. After a few days of observation, they announced who they were and that they now wanted to leave. The shocked medical staff told them, "No, no! You need to stay. You guys really do have some major problems."

Imagine going in normal and coming out with issues!

Although the above example is somewhat humorous in nature, my thought at the time was: *How can a group of healthy people be so easily labelled as mentally unstable?* All I wanted was to help people feel better fast, without assuming anything except that they can get better. I became frustrated and confused, much like those students mentally going in one way and coming out another. When my initial intentions of helping others collided with the reality of the academic courses and concepts, as presented to me in class, I became disillusioned and didn't want to do anything more in the field of psychology; especially, if that was the way it was done.

Little did I realize how ingrained my desire would remain in natural human behaviour.

Don't get we wrong, psychology can be helpful and more than just a necessity. I simply find it fascinating that many therapists now want me to teach them the ideas I've discovered really work; coincidentally, that aren't taught in psych classes or schools anywhere. I have worked with medical doctors, social workers, psychologists, and many others trained in their specialty; yet discovered, like me, they couldn't find the answers they were seeking. Coming out of university, I believed I couldn't help anyone if I felt confused by the solutions I'd be offering them. For the individual wanting to feel better, it's very difficult when the only answer given to them is frustrating at best, and not needed in the least. Unfortunately, for most people, their options are usually limited to setting up an appointment with someone you're "supposed" to go to and doing what they tell you to do. The problem is the so-called professional is limited by what they know and can only apply what they've learned.

Even when I wasn't thinking behaviour, everything I thought was rooted in some sort of action and reaction. I couldn't get away from it. It seemed to surround me and I never lost my fascination with it.

Think about this: Every person you talk to begins an interaction that can be a quick passing, an informal information sharing session, or even a life changing "chance" meeting, that can change the lives of both parties forever. If we were only more open to others and their knowledge, everything changes. I will soon recount an event that changed the course of my life and after reading and applying the lessons of this book, will hopefully change yours too.

We also must remember that not all such interactions are favourable or desired. We need to learn how to accept the ones that will do us good and understand how to reject, eliminate, and neutralize the ones that won't benefit us, which in many cases even cause us harm.

When I was not "officially" in this profession, it is now obvious to me that I really was always in it, without actually knowing it. I would talk people through things, helping them with their issues whenever I could. People would "find" me (chance meetings!) and I would help. I didn't require a total family history, have to speak about their parents, or have them come back for repeated visits (although many did return to talk and reflect, which made them feel better after we met).

This was something I would do in casual meetings and interactions with people. I always knew when things weren't right and I had an uncanny natural ability to know what and why. Some call it a sixth sense or intuition. Whatever its name, it is a strong feeling I've learned to trust and listen to, and so can you.

As I reflect back now, it's clearer to figure out why I could do what I did. That's why they say hindsight is 20/20. It's always easier after the events occur. There are exceptions to this rule, as in cases of trauma or deep rooted emotional events, when memories can be so innate that these thoughts play like a looped video. The end of the memory is connected to its beginning and it plays over and over. I have developed an amazing process and program to "unloop" memories, so that people traumatized by anything in their past can be freed to live in the present without those old recurring past fears. The material in this book is something I use with everyone I work with, as thoughts and thinking are what get people in trouble in the first place. Negative thinking often occurs before any other negative events ever happen. Some of the events I am talking about are trauma. I'm referring to events that would be so severe a person wouldn't be able to concentrate enough to be reading this right now. They'd be totally overwhelmed, almost incapacitated. Yes, I even have something for that situation. All recurring memories work like that. It is the same way a trauma works, but without the severity and the debilitation.

So, back to my story.

While managing one of my retail stores, a relative came to me very distraught and at their wit's end. Her daughter was having incredible difficulty with school. There were so many issues, from separation anxiety, fears, phobias, and more. This innocent young girl was in her early grades and no one could help. Her mother visited the school and spoke with the teachers and principal, without success. Next, she turned to the school board and received no answers. The sad journey continued to her doctor, who led her to psychologists, psychiatrists, and more, all without results. The little girl became withdrawn, anxious, and hated going to school. Every day the mother would have to pry herself away after bringing her daughter to the start of class. It was heartbreaking, as they were both victims of this suffering.

On this particular morning at my store, the mother was shaking and on the verge of tears, worrying about her little girl's future. This fateful day was more than coincidental, but necessary in the direction of both our lives. While hearing her plight, I'm sure she thought I'd sit there, listen, and then give heart-warming moral support, just as so many others had before me. I mean really, what do you say to someone who has thoroughly followed all the proper procedures and asked all the right questions of all the right people?

Fortunately for her, that is just not my style!

What came next was a shocker for both of us. I said without hesitation, "I know exactly what's wrong with her. I can fix her in 30 days!" This beleaguered mother was ecstatic. She had hope in her eyes, because for the first time she'd been told there was another option. This was an exciting life changing journey for me as well. I was suddenly on a mission and someone's life depended on me.

Later that same day, interesting things began to happen and I didn't understand how or why. In the afternoon, I was running errands when a detour sidetracked me, putting me on an unfamiliar road in an unknown part of town outside of Detroit. Not a place to be lost. As I was looking for a place to turn around, I noticed this small used bookstore that seemed to be drawing me towards it. I soon entered this cozy and welcoming place, where there just so happened to be many self-help books in stock. I knew right then this stop was part of my mission and had happened without consciously trying to find it. I was also certain that whatever was going on back home in this little girl's mind and body was totally unconscious. My years of university studies hadn't prepared me for this moment. This feeling I was experiencing was new and special. The stakes were higher and the quality of this child's life hung in the balance. Yet the real difference was it was happening right at that moment, with everything coming together without trying. Pieces of the puzzle were effortlessly fitting into place. The bookshelves dealing with change surrounded me. As I looked through various titles and found some particular processes, my book pile began to grow. Finally after several hours of research, I walked out with ten books! This was more than any semester at university.

As I drove home, I was very excited because I knew I now possessed the answers. Now all I had to do was put them together, to fit the needs of this young girl.

What transpired after that bookstore visit was a deep quest for knowledge and a thirst for answers. I knew there was a solution and was determined to find it. I put together a program to change this child's thinking and her perception of her perceived world. A technique that would reprogram her inner voice and thought processes was the only solution. My mission was to remove her irrational thinking that was not rational reasoning. She was reacting to her situations opposite to her desires. Her wires were crossed, but were they really? Based on what she knew and her point of reference, they really weren't. Her reality was her reality. It simply didn't merge with the reality of daily living and functioning of other people she needed to "blend in with" and please. After putting into practice a set of instructions and subconscious reprogramming techniques, the wheel of change began to move. Wow, did it ever move quickly! I was able to modify her sense of reality by changing the quality of her thoughts. Once her thoughts changed, her thinking changed, and her life changed forever.

Within two weeks, this girl was walking into the school by herself and waving goodbye to her mother, as if she'd never had a separation problem. She now looked forward to school and it became fun. A side benefit from this transformation was that for the first time her parents were able to go on a vacation on their own.

Not only were these results not feasible before, it was beyond the realm of possibility. Why is it that I could figure this out and others could not? Was it due to the fact I didn't apply conventional methods or my beliefs were different than the self-styled professionals? Perhaps it was that I identified with the girl's pain and was compelled to find a unique solution. There was no trying or attempting. My goal was to succeed without having to know how I would do it. It didn't matter how, only that I did it.

Whatever it was, I was more concerned with the outcome than the process. Most researchers are into theory, so that they can duplicate the results. The only problem is that when you always see the same results, you expect those same ones over and over. That means if you're used to not seeing results or results take a long time, results will not be possible or they'll always take a long time!

None of the educational professionals this family consulted thought changes were possible. Based on their belief, they were right that this girl couldn't change; therefore, their techniques did not work. On the other hand, my attitude was different. I anticipated this girl could change. I didn't care that the others couldn't fix her. What was important to me was there was a desire, a belief, and most important, an expectancy. These three things together are capable of whatever you wish.

It has been proven that people will get better in direct relation to the attitude of the attending physician or therapist. If in need of help regarding your physical or emotional health, do yourself a favour and seek another opinion if your care giver doesn't believe their methods will work in your situation.

I trust you are reading this book to create some changes in your life. I encourage you to have hope. I encourage you to open your mind. I encourage you to bring back those forgotten dreams and live them. Anything is possible. To think otherwise is a waste. Follow along and I'll show you some very powerful techniques that work quickly and for the long term. These techniques will change your life forever.

I once told a client, "I believe anything is possible." He made a weird face and countered, "You want me to believe that if I were to stand on a hilltop and spread my arms that I could fly?" Without missing a beat or losing eye contact with him I replied, "Why do you think planes were invented?"

Jacques Cousteau was a great ocean explorer. He looked under the sea and wanted to swim like a fish. He never said he wanted to be a fish. However, he did find a way to breathe under water by scuba diving.

We may not develop wings or grow gills but we don't need to either. It's when we assume that we need to grow wings and develop gills we get into trouble.

There are many ways to accomplish similar things. If we think there's only one way, we may conclude that it just isn't doable. The reality is anything is possible when there is hope and desire. It may not happen today, it may not happen tomorrow, but it will happen in the future. You need to hang onto that thought. It will create great things and accomplish so much, while others linger in their disillusionment.

When something doesn't work, it doesn't mean it's not achievable, only that you need to try a different approach. I'm always fascinated when someone tells me things are not possible. Everything has possibility, if there's a sliver of hope.

I have seen this many times when there's a health issue and a person has been advised there's nothing more that can be done. What the attending caregiver really means is that based on their limited scope of knowledge, they don't know what to do. It doesn't signify there are no other options. If the client believes there are no options, they lose all hope. Take away a person's hopes and dreams and you take away their life.

As I mentioned previously, isn't it true that the more we know, the more we realize how little we know?

In this book, I will breakdown some barriers and share with you some incredible ways to create change. If you allow me, I will open your mind to possibilities - your possibilities. Just imagine being able to overcome negative thinking and thoughts. For many people, life would be quite different and be immensely and immediately more enjoyable.

I don't care how old or how young you are. It doesn't matter how lucky or out of luck you think you are. It doesn't matter what's currently happening in your life or what's occurred in your past. It really doesn't matter. Honestly, I have seen so many people who've told me I was there last hope and by using my processes, they all changed! Problems from 10, 20, 30, 50 and even 75 years earlier, were now suddenly disappearing. Issues no one thought would ever go away … rapidly gone. It didn't matter how skeptical, negative, or anxious a person was in the beginning; when there was a desire to make things change, change came relatively easily.

Becoming aware is a powerful and empowering moment in anyone's life. It's like waking from a sound sleep. Becoming conscious of the possibilities and the powerful person you are, will set you free from all your limitations. Choice is a wonderful thing that's powerful in its possession, but debilitating if someone feels they have none.

Let's practice some awareness. Right now, you see that we're sharing a moment together and thinking exactly the same thoughts. I am speaking directly to you as a new friend who you are allowing into your life. That's right; we are in the same place at the same time.

Welcome to the world of awareness! In these thoughts and this thinking there will only be possibilities. Let's look at what we can do to remove the limitations of old thoughts and thinking; thus, freeing ourselves to become everything we can be. In other words, we will look at eliminating the stress of the past and create a future we can now look forward to living.

Things are about to get much better!

"It is the mark of an educated mind to be able to entertain a thought without accepting it."
Aristotle

Chapter Two

Stress!

Making Happiness Your Choice

Have You Unknowingly Accepted Stress As a Part of Your Life?

Stress is an interesting word that means different things to different people. One of the first questions I ask clients is, "How's your stress?" which results in some very interesting answers. Some quickly state, "It's high! That's why I'm here today," while a few say, "I'm handling it." Others declare, "Well everyone has stress," or, "It's no more than average."

What is the average stress that you're supposed to have? What is the acceptable level? What are the warning signs there's too much stress in your life? What happens if you don't do anything about it? What happens if you think that it's normal and acceptable to have stress because everyone else seems to have it too?

The first thing we need to do is define the word "stress" and try to get a handle on it. In most people's lives, stress is covered up in the all-encompassing explanation that, "It's the pressures of everyday life." The dictionary definition of stress is "to exert force or pressure."

When someone pulls on a chain, they're exerting stress on it. However, if you exert too much stress the chain will break. That's right, too much stress past a certain point and there'll be a breakdown. Manufacturers rate a chain's strength based on the pressure that can be exerted before it breaks. They can determine exactly when the chain will snap, but can't tell you which link will break first. When a person is stressed, their chain of life and well-being is being stressed. Now imagine each link of this chain. Let's say there are 1000's of them, each representing a bodily system, a piece of your health puzzle. This is why almost any illness or disease has its roots in stress. The pressure or stress that one feels in their of life.

It's estimated that 80-90% of all doctor visits are rooted in stress. I personally believe it's even higher. It is becoming more prevalent to receive health care for stress related problems, illnesses, or symptoms. Unfortunately, it's now so common, it's almost becoming accepted. This is something we need to not accept. Stress related symptoms do need to be addressed and corrected, but we can't simply forget why the symptoms occurred in the first place, if we want to prevent other issues from showing up. If we only work with the symptoms of the problem and correct those, there's nothing preventing other symptoms occurring based on the same original issue. I have seen this time and again. It is though we're in the business of chasing symptoms, like a child chasing butterflies. There are other options and solutions. Let's try and understand stress first, so we don't have to be so accepting of it. After we understand it, it'll be easier to slay this potentially deadly, energy-draining disease causing dragon.

Speed and Efficiency - Society Stressing Us Out

In today's society everything is about speed and efficiency. It's no wonder people are stressed. The internet is a wonderful tool connecting us to the world. Even it has sped up over time: dial up to high speed to cable and satellite. You can't go back, it's very difficult. If you return to dial up service after experiencing high speed, you're apt to want to throw your computer out a window. This applies to other conveniences we take for granted today. For example, when you put something in the microwave for 30 seconds, you might take it out with 10 seconds left because it just isn't fast enough.

It wasn't all that long ago there were no microwaves, cell phones, or computers. Things have changed very quickly since the 1980's and 1990's.

Where does it end and will it ever? Don't count on it. As I write this, a new iPhone was released for sale. I'm sure this will seem like some time ago because technology waits for no one. Customers stood in line for hours because they want more and more technology. All around us things are getting faster and faster. Some of you might be overwhelmed, while others such as those camped out overnight to be the first to get that new phone, are obviously not. Their desire is for the speed of the future. For some, this scenario causes stress trying to cope with constant change, while others can't wait to experience it.

To better understand these polar opposites, we have to ask one basic question:

Is Stress Real or Perceived?

It's a proven fact that "perceived" stress and "actual" stress have the same affect in the body and mind. Stress breaks down the body at a deep cellular level, whether it's something current or projected. Many think that it shouldn't bother someone if it isn't real, yet this is wrong; reality and vivid imagination have exactly the same effect on your body. That's why anxiety is so troubling, as it's a perceived fear and in most cases, you become anxious about being anxious. Our thought processes are very important. If a perceived fear has the same effect as an actual event, doesn't that mean that perceived safety would have the same effect as safety? Just an idea. Think about it. This is why positive thinkers are not anxious. It's an oxymoron. It isn't possible to be anxious if you are thinking positive thoughts. This is the basis of what will be taught in later chapters and how to create the change in one's thoughts, and therefore their reality. We have great success in all of our anxiety programs, both in the office and online, because we have unlocked the ways of changing thoughts and thinking. Remember, reality exists inside your head. Change your thoughts, change your thinking, watch the emotional responses change, and you will regain your life.

For many of you this will be the first time you'll be in control of your thoughts and your thinking. It will be an exciting time and a life changing empowering experience.

Doing Something About Stress

One thing that's certain is this: If we don't do something about being overwhelmed by events going on around us, it's possible to get pulled into an emotional whirlpool of issues, problems, and other pressures, while just trying to survive each day.

This is the stress we call life.

Stress is relative to what we know, as well as what we don't think we know. What is known is that over the years, as things get quicker and there are more burdens on us, we place additional demands on ourselves.

The interesting aspect is that this is understandable. People comprehend stress and how it makes them feel; however, we don't need to accept it. Here we are on the merry-go-round of life and it's all fine and dandy, until it starts going faster and faster to the point it's moving so quickly you can't get off. Stress has been around for a long, long time. In fact, stress has been present for as long as human beings have walked this earth.

My theory is stress isn't the "events," but rather what we perceive happened or might happen in the future.

It's all about your thoughts and what you are thinking.

The events are not as stressful as the thoughts themselves.

The solutions lay in our ability to understand our thoughts, as we progress through Thought Shifting learning to change our thinking. It's never too late to learn to be happy. When you learn to change your thoughts, it will change your thinking and your life forever. Happiness will be more than a possibility; it'll be your conscious choice.

I asked a 35-year-old client suffering from 25 years of anxiety a simple question: "Of all the things that you've ever worried about during the past two and a half decades, which ones ever came true?" He stopped, his eyes slowly shifting around the room in every direction and finally replied, "Nothing."

This is usually the case. Our greatest fears are of things that'll never happen. It's a perceived fear of the unknown. It isn't the unknown that we should be afraid of; it's the stuff we know. If you didn't know what you know, you wouldn't feel the way you feel. It's all the past experiences that have you worried about the future. The key is to be able to refocus what we desire on demand, instead of projecting the fears of the past into the future.

I will explain some of that now, but more in a later chapter and it gets so much better!

In my clinic I have worked with stressed clients ranging from a 3-year-old to a 90-year-old. The child was anxious because someone said something about her in preschool, while the 90-year-old was described by her younger 89-year-old brother as being negative and frazzled her entire life. He brought her into the office after I helped him.

It isn't necessarily what happens to a person, but more about what they think happened or should have happened.

Why is it that the same event can occur to two different people and you get two different results? Several years ago, I was helping coach my son's hockey team. They were probably 12 years old. Upon losing a close game, the coach chewed the players out. Afterwards, I remember watching the kids walking out of the dressing room, all with different reactions to this tirade. In particular, I recall two teammates exiting at the same time, with one child exhibiting anger and talking under his breath, while his teammate came out crying.

The way we process a situation will depend on how we perceive it. You only know what you know. You can't be expected to know anything else. All our experiences come directly or indirectly through our environment, parents, friends, teachers, media, etc., and have a tangible effect as to how we react or not.

It's intriguing when I have so many people coming to see me for many different, yet similar issues. For some, a particular life stressor is debilitating, while for another the same issue is easily handled. We are so used to comparing ourselves to others that we also stress ourselves out over not handling a situation we think we should.

As we become more independent to our own actions and reactions, the healthier we will become. This doesn't mean you don't have to care about others. Instead, remember that you must first care for yourself in order to help others. It's like when the airplane flight crew instructs you if the cabin pressure changes and the oxygen masks fall down, that you're to put yours on first before helping anyone else.

This whole process will allow you to get better, so you can then help others. By controlling and eliminating stress in your life, everything changes.

You may not be aware that the word "stress" is rather new. It's hard to imagine it's only been in the last 50 years or so that it was officially recognized or "discovered." That doesn't mean it was immediately accepted and treated for what it is. We've come a long way, but also have a very long way to go.

Hungarian researcher Hans Selye coined the term as he attempted to describe the effects of "strain" on the body. It was sometime later when he admitted that had his English been better, he'd have named it "strain" instead of "stress." Interestingly, prior to Selye's coining the term, the word "stress" cannot be found in any other cultures. It seems there really was no word in any language to describe strain on the body.

With stress being so new, it's no wonder people don't talk about it much and many still act like it doesn't exist. Now, visualize finding a weed or perhaps one tiny caterpillar in a beautiful garden. Do we leave it alone and pretend it's okay? Well, I suppose you would if you didn't know the dangers or the repercussions. Perhaps you were told to ignore it and it would go away. It's possible that might happen, but not likely. Our past experiences tell us what happens when you don't take care of your garden. We know what occurs if you let a weed or a parasite live off your garden. Then again, if you went to a professional who said it's normal and acceptable behaviour, we would follow their advice.

Stress Issues Have Become Accepted But Don't You Accept Them!

The problem with stress is it's still this new label, which has a new emphasis. It's been like a revelation. In the past, you were either normal or mental. There was no real grey area. People would laugh behind others' backs if they showed anxiety, depression, or even phobias. The mind was always a deep abyss and no one knew what was on the bottom, or even if there was a bottom. It was scary and frightening; people who suffered from accumulated stress were deemed "crazy" and often put away in some medical ward. Today, it's more common for these same individuals to go off work for stress or "personal issues."

It's great that you can finally get a reprieve or break to catch your breath and hopefully find the answers to what's really happening in your life.

Stress shows up with warning signs and symptoms, which can either be heeded or ignored. If we pay attention and do something about them, there's a good possibility it will be a limited issue or problem.

There is a small variable that will make or break the end result. It depends on who you seek help from and what they tell you to do or not to do. More and more people are realizing the importance of first getting the information they need, then using this knowledge to make an educated decision on how to proceed. There might be occasions when you feel overwhelmed and don't know what to do or whom to turn to. My advice is always to seek help at the highest level. Then when you're in a better position, keep looking for answers to your particular situation. Your goal is to live your life as stress free as possible. Keep in mind, it doesn't matter if it is "real" or "perceived," it means the same because it has the same end result.

Whenever I hear the line, "This might sound crazy, but...," I reply, "It doesn't matter if anyone else thinks it's real, if it's in your head then it is real." Reality only exists inside our head. I get a big kick out of clients all upset because their doctor advised them, "It's all in your head." I tell them, "Well of course it is! If it wasn't in your head, it wouldn't be a problem, would it?" In other words, if you didn't think it was a problem, would it be a problem? You probably wouldn't have made a doctor's appointment. This is something we will work more on. Once we learn to control thoughts and thinking, everything will change.

Our perception is our projection. If we perceive a situation with a history of stress attached to it, that's what we'll see, hear, and feel when a trigger to the memory appears.

I was writing a part of this book while camping. The sun was setting, the pit fire was crackling in the background, and I could feel its warmth. It's relaxing just thinking about it. It's been my experience that people are their most resourceful when they're relaxed. Yet, a middle-aged man passing our site stopped in his tracks to tell me to put away my laptop because

I was camping. I had to laugh, as to me, this was a relaxing pastime. I was writing and reflecting about stress reduction. It was a great place to be. So remember, what's relaxing to someone else doesn't have to be relaxing to you and vice versa.

When you find what you enjoy doing, don't worry about what others think. Enjoy the moment and its effect on your future perceptions.

It's remarkable that so many people talk about stress as if it's as acceptable as life itself. It may be common and all around us, but it doesn't have to be accepted as something we must live with on a daily basis. Life is all about options and opportunities to create the changes we desire. Change starts in our minds. Unfortunately, stress changes any scenario, because it breaks things down by its very nature. It is vital to do everything to avoid and minimize stress, and never give up finding a solution that's workable for you and your situation.

As you continue to move forward in this book, you'll discover many new ways that will help create positive change in your life. Over the years, I have worked with thousands of people. Through their experiences, as well as your own, you will now learn how to handle and manage thoughts and thinking; therefore, you will easily begin to handle and manage any stress and your whole life.

"The mind is everything.
What you think you become."
Buddha

Chapter Three

Stress

Is It Real Or Just All In Your Head?
What Do You Believe?

That's a good question. On one hand, you wouldn't feel stressed if there was no one else around to distress or remind you of your pain. On the other hand, there is the old saying, "No one can upset you without your permission." So, are you openly and outright granting your permission? Probably not. Then what is it? It's sort of like when clients say they're "realists" who don't want to become too hopeful in case things don't work out. I reply with, "Well what if they do work out? That was a huge waste of time when you could have been living a reality of happiness and great expectations." Interesting, right? I follow up by asking, "What is reality?" For a negative person, their reality is focusing on things they don't want to happen. Conversely, a positive person is always focusing on things they do want to have happen. That's the only difference. It's realizing your reality is your thinking and your thinking becomes your reality. Changing your thinking changes everything.

Reality is the perception of what YOU think will most likely happen. It sounds more like a projection to me. That takes us down to the fact that the perception is really projection. So then, is reality in essence your projected perception of a situation? In other words, your reality is what your limited thoughts and thinking are letting you believe is possible or not possible. Now it's getting deep but follow it and reread it if need be, until you fully understand the full meaning.

It now appears our thoughts are what we project, based on what we believe is or isn't possible, but is THAT reality? It is in our own limited world. We call that our "map" of the world. Our private little world, but our map is really not "the territory." The territory is reality, which only exists in our own minds. That's why no two minds are exactly alike. We may agree or disagree on some of the same things, yet eventually we certainly will not agree. This is because our realities are different.

Now, why are realities different between people, and often between siblings who shared much of the same environment growing up? We tend to accumulate our own style of thoughts and thinking. Some good, some bad, and some rather ugly. This becomes our map and our own sense of what's real and what's not. Our map is our escape route, our roadway into the future. It is important to understand our own limitations, so we can become limitless. On several occasions, I have spoken to people who were able to overcome huge obstacles and when asked how they were able to accomplish such a feat they reply, "I didn't know I wasn't supposed to be able to do it."

This is also now playing into beliefs, which is the most powerful characteristic of a person because it sets everything else in motion. There is something admirable to be said about a powerful belief system. Some individuals believe they can climb mountains and they do, as others believe they can't leave their houses and they don't. Your belief is what you think it is. It's all a thought and where do thoughts live? Where do they actually come from?

Actually, you have to admit that it really is all in your head, which remember, isn't a bad thing. To be told something "was in your head" used to be a very negative statement, as if some terrible serious illness. This couldn't be farther from the truth. Yet, nothing means anything if it isn't in your head. Your sense of reality is based on your thoughts that exist only in your mind that lives in your head.

I remember when my daughter was young and in the early years of grade school. She was very upset and stressed out. One day I sat with her and asked, "What is wrong?" She hesitantly told me that another student at school had said something about her. I then asked, "If someone says something to you and you think it's a problem, is it a problem?" She replied, "Yes, it is." I then asked her, "If someone is not saying anything about you but you think they are, do you have a problem?" to which she answered, "Yes." Finally, I inquired, "If someone is talking about you but you don't think there is a problem, is there a problem?" She then replied, "No."

Even a young child knows that if you don't think it's a problem, it isn't. Alternatively, if you believe things are problems and negativity is your most common mindset, you'll think up so many negative issues you'll become a prisoner of your own thoughts. That's what Thought Shifting is all about; to not only give you a key to your mental prison, but to teach you how to stay out of it. It's a type of mental retraining and education that will free you forever.

"You feel good, you feel bad, and these feelings are bubbling from your own unconsciousness, from your own past. Nobody is responsible except you. Nobody can make you angry, and nobody can make you happy."
Osho

Chapter Four

The Real Problem:

Understanding It So You Can Treat It Once and For All

At a conference I once heard a guest speaker say something quite interesting. He started his speech saying that there are many "isms" of the world that have caused unrest, such as communism, terrorism, racism, alcoholism, and several others. He went on to say the real problem and the most destructive of all "isms" is *negativism*. This really got my attention, as I've been teaching that same message for years!

It's not that these other issues don't cause stress and emotional issues on their own. Of course they do. Anyone that's been personally affected by the above-mentioned "isms", would have experienced an extreme amount of negativism; therefore, an extreme amount of stress would have occurred.

I think we can all agree that negativity breeds stress. If you don't believe me, let me explain a simple process that will remove all doubt. There is a process called "muscle testing" which tests the strength of an isolated muscle group to show the affect of things, usually products, on the body. It is often used by a person who believes they're sensitive to something and their body reacts negatively to it by becoming weakened. A common way of doing this is an arm extension, where you're told to hold your arm straight out from your body. You then hold the arm in place with a sturdy resistance, as someone gently applies pressure against the arm to show its steadiness and even muscle strength. Then when you place a substance in their hand that the individual is sensitive to, the body strength would visibly weaken when the muscle is tested again.

This also holds true with thoughts. If I have you think of a positive thought or someone/something you care about, you will test "strong" on the muscle resistance. If I then have you think about someone or something that you don't like, you will test "weak" and your muscle strength will be substantially diluted.It is an amazing process that holds true with everyone I have ever demonstrated it on. When a person has a negative thought, their body goes weak. No matter what muscle you were to test, it would be weaker if a person focuses on anything negative or perceived as such.

Now let's try and understand this. If a negative thought can reduce the body's energy, think of all the health issues that could develop! Think of it this way: if an animal in the wild has a low energy level, what happens to it? It becomes prey. It might just get sick and break down unable to eat, at which point it could easily be attacked and eventually killed.

Unknowingly, we too often allow our bodies to weaken and break down. Sadly, people are becoming so involved in the symptoms of stress, there's little focus on the actual causes of the stress itself.

This muscle test gets even more surprising and reveals even more. Not only do negative thoughts make you test "weak," but so does ANY negative statement that you say.

That's right, ANYTHING you say.

That means any remark that leaves your lips. It doesn't matter if you're kidding or joking or trying to be funny. Many people have these negative little "cutesy" sayings. Well, guess what? They aren't helping the cause. They are making you weak, stressing your systems, contributing to poor health, and destabilizing the immune system.

Furthermore, if someone says anything negative to you, your muscles will test weak. That's right, you don't even have to believe in what they're saying, nor do you have to be directly engaged in the conversation. You will become weakened. This includes watching TV, especially the news. Reading the paper is another terrible one we will talk more in depth about later. It also includes your negative partner and all those negative relatives!

And you thought it was just you? No, it isn't. Remember, you've had a lot of help getting stressed out. This information will help you understand it and work with it.

To recap: It's what you say, what you think, and what you surround yourself with that will either bring you up or bring you down. It will either make you stronger or make you weaker. Everything affects you, EVERYTHING. This is at a deep subconscious level; in many cases, it's pretty obvious consciously as well.

Think of all the situations and the resulting strain on the body! Negativity from **your** words and **your** thoughts, plus **their** words has exactly the same result on the body. It completely weakens your body and drains your energy. In order to keep up your body's energy, your immunity, and your overall future outlook, you must be made aware of several things that need to change. You could say there are things you need to stop doing, as well as things you will begin doing.

Things You Say But Really Don't Mean

People don't realize that the body believes every word you say. That's right, every word you say your body takes literally. That's a scary thought for most of us. Imagine if everything you said in conversation was taken exactly as it was said!

This is what occurs when you say negative statements. Even though you don't mean it, aren't serious or intend any harm, this is NOT how the body interprets things.

It is a proven fact those negative clichés that many people say actually manifest themselves into physical problems. I have seen it time in and time out at my clinic.

People who say things like, "I can't see it" often wear glasses. Those who say, "It's a pain in the neck" will have neck and back pain. There are so many statements people say, but don't mean to actually happen. I like to express it this way: If you don't want it to be true, DON'T SAY IT. What you say, you picture and what you picture, you attract. You must understand that thoughts have an incredible power. As you speak words, you picture thoughts. When that happens, there's an incredible attraction that takes place. If you say negative things and negative things happen, according to your mind, you are successful! It doesn't matter what the intention was to say, it's what you actually said. It's more than what you are "just saying" to others; it becomes what you're actually saying to yourself.

You may be questioning, "How am I going to stop all this from happening?" Remember, the information I'm going to be giving you will explain how to create these changes. For the time being, I am explaining the concepts before the actual techniques. That is what's different about this material. I will be giving you step-by-step techniques to create these changes. There are many self-help books, videos, and programs that will recommend that you should change and what you will get when you change. However, most leave out one simple little thing: how to actually create self change and what to actually do. Our programs take another approach; whereby, you'll see the difference in a new inner voice and the feelings that will follow.

So let's get back to the processes!

Many people say things that they don't or didn't literally mean. Look at it this way: The brain is considered more powerful than the most powerful computers. In fact, the brain is often referred to as the body's computer. Take a calculator for instance, which is a tiny computer for calculations. You punch in some numbers and solutions so exact and precise immediately come up. Now, if you jokingly put in a bunch of random numbers, would you be surprised by the end result? Of course not, because what you put in, you get out. The same applies with the things that you say.

Sometimes people say negative things to others with the hope that someone will come back and correct them with a compliment instead. An example might be saying how bad they look in a certain outfit to their friends. The hope is that the friend will instead say how great they look.

It doesn't always play that way. Years ago, a client came to me with a fear of public speaking. I explained that he should not say anything negative to anyone else that he didn't want to be true or come true. This young man totally agreed and wanted to tell me a story. I love stories. He related talking to a buddy about his fear of successfully giving an important upcoming work presentation. Without hesitation, his funny friend laughed and replied, "Yeah, you'll probably mess it up!" As my client explained, it wasn't the reaction he thought he'd get, and it certainly wasn't what he wanted to hear.

I often say, "If you don't want your head cut off, keep it off the chopping block." Once again, if you don't want it to be true, DON'T SAY IT. If you wouldn't write it down as a goal, don't say it. Our processes will allow you to begin catching yourself stating negative things, as you correct what you say with what you actually want to say. The great thing is what you truly want and consistently say will eventually happen. Let's get into some specifics and how to properly apply these new concepts.

The best practice of this technique is listening to what others are saying around you. You'll become aware of the things people are actually creating in their lives and become conscious of what you say on a day-to-day basis. This is very important to understand, as you take it into your world by practicing and interacting with others. This is really where the fun begins. As serious as this material is, my clients start having a lot of fun when they apply this method to their daily life.

Awareness is necessary to open you up for change. However, your action of using these techniques will make the change happen, becoming part of your every day transformation. The nice thing about what I have in store for you is the instructions and techniques that are simple and easy to follow.

When it comes to talking and saying things, the next logical question should be. . .

What Should You Say?

Telling you what NOT to do is easy. You've been hearing that your whole life. The trick is knowing what to say to keep your energy up, allowing you to feel as good as you should be. This is what Thought Shifting is all about. Maximizing your thoughts, to maximize feeling great as often as possible, is your new game plan. You should never want to turn down an opportunity to feel fantastic. Why would you want to do something as silly as that? Yet, that's what you do every time you open your mouth to say something either in response to a topic, or when simply greeting a person known or new to you.

The truth is there are opportunities to set the mood, tempo, and how YOU want to feel. When you do it correctly, the added bonus is that it also affects other people in a positive way. On the flipside, if done incorrectly, you will influence them in a negative way.

What You Choose Is Your Decision

It's always a decision.

In the past, you never knew you had a choice, so how could you have made them? Now we're learning the difference and how to create it, as we desire it. Powerful stuff when you know how to use it.

If every time you say something to someone it affects your body energy, it's important to feel as good as possible, every time possible. Family, friends, and co-workers are always asking, "How are you doing?" or "How's it going?" These causal formalities seem innocent enough, but your response to a simple question is far more complicated than you realize.

It is interesting when you realize the brain is always trying to give you what it believes you really desire. It gets this information from what it thinks are your requests. The requests come from the things that you "innocently" say, but don't really mean. It also comes from inner thoughts and your environment, which we'll discuss soon.

What you say, you picture and what you picture, you attract. It's that simple. There is an old saying that warns, "Be careful what you wish for." The truth is that it's deeper than just that. It's actually, "Be careful of what you say and what you think of." These sayings become your thoughts and are then attracted into your life.

For some, your mouths are probably open as you begin to realize how you've been attracting your own negativity. Others are wondering, "How can it be this simple?" I recently had a new client in my office and we started talking about thoughts, awareness, and changing thoughts and thinking. She told me how she'd already started doing that on her own, but in a manner other than what I was explaining to her. I asked, "Is it working?" and her instant reply was, "NO!" She recognized the need to change her thoughts, yet she was doing it all wrong. Intention is one thing. Technique is something else. Only proper techniques will take your intention to the change you desire and keep it changed. It's very important to recognize the need for a proper technique, which will in fact change your thought processes and energy levels. Trust me, this stuff works if you let it. You need to use it, so you can let it work. Follow it and it will give you the results that I have witnessed in countless clients over the years.

Let's break this down: If we rate from 1 to 10 (with 10 being the highest) how you want to be feeling, what would you say? Most of us would say 10. I agree. There's plenty of room at the top and it's very crowded down low. Let's look at a comparison of how this rating works. Say you want to purchase an item that costs $10, but you only have $5. Can you buy it? Well, no. If you had $8 or even $9.50, you still can't get it, because $10 is $10. The point I am making is if you want to feel like a 10, you have to start talking like a 10.

Your Attraction Strategy Starts With The Words You Use

When you ask people how they're doing, their responses usually fall into the category of, "Not bad," (remember the mind cannot process a negative and sees this as "BAD – not") or they reply with some other "less than a 10" reply. Like we've already learned, you can't be a 10 if you're talking like a 5. In fact, many responses aren't even a 5. When I ask clients what they think a response of "Not bad" would be on a scale from 1 to 10, they often think it's a 6 or 7! I find this funny, as it's more like a 2 or 3.

Let's gain a better understanding of a few basics. There is so much negativity around us and inbred in us, we need to look at the bigger picture. The truth is we are quite lucky people. Most of us live in places where we have the freedom to buy and read books. We live in a world of cell phones, microwave ovens, laptops, and personal computers. We own cars or have good public transportation to get around. We have goals, dreams, and desires that make up our future. We have a standard of living that has never been better in the world. Many of us live with better conveniences than royalty had available to them not so long ago.

Most of us have or have had relationships, family, children or grandchildren, siblings, teachers, mentors, friends, neighbours, and all the lessons and experiences that go along with them.

We have health or perhaps youthfulness, eyesight, hearing, and so many basics that countless people do not have. We also take many things for granted. I believe the characteristics we need to all share are HOPE and DESIRE. This means you are looking forward to the future and you have dreams and ambitions.

In the big picture, you really are doing GREAT. If you think of how lucky you really are, your response to a question like, "How are you?" would result in a totally different answer than is usually the norm.

REMEMBER: People are NOT asking you, "How is your Biggest Problem?"

The answer you give needs to be understood as something that's positive in your life. After years of negativity, internally and externally, it's not uncommon for people to forget how great things really are. We must realize that in the midst of negativity, there are still great times, great memories, and great opportunities. If nothing else, why is it that when a person asks how you are, automatically it's as if they're asking you about your worst problem? This is what most people do, which results in immediately feeling bad.

This is going to stop. This is also something that's easy to quickly change.

As you better understand how this process works, you will begin to create energy within yourself to feel better every time you open your mouth. It is no longer going to be about what people ask you; instead, it will be how you decide you want to feel, which in turn will decide how you will respond.

Focusing on What You Want – To Get What You Desire

The key is figuring out what you want to focus on. This applies each time you're asked the simple question, "How are you?", "How's it going?", "What's new?", or anything else someone says to you. The goal is to realize that things really are better than you have allowed yourself to believe. You also need to focus on how you want things to be in the future. When you do this, you are speaking the truth and you aren't making anything up. People do this in different ways.

It is all about finding and focusing on any joy in your life. Some think of their families, others about relationships, or perhaps where and how they live. They realize things really are GREAT in the big picture. We all know people who seem so upbeat when you encounter them and wonder, "Can they really be that happy?" Maybe they've read this book or taken one of my courses. Some may be projecting their happiness without realizing why they do it. They just know it feels good. Many people say the right things but don't understand them. You, my friend, will be able to use it, understand it, and benefit from it.

What I want for you is to be feeling good as often as possible. The way to do this is to answer people in the most positive way possible. This is actually quite easy when you consider how lucky you really are and how great life really is for you.

Your replies to anyone speaking to you, especially in a meet and greet situation, should always be with the understanding that "what you say, you picture and what you picture, you attract." As a result, your response to, "How are you?" will be, "GREAT!" or "Awesome!" or even "Fantastic!"

You Can Never Be Better Than Whatever You Say

Remember, you cannot be better than what you say. It's been proven that your body's energy level goes either up or down, depending on what you say. It's that easy and it's THAT important. Too many people blow off the above responses, believing they are insignificant. These types of greetings are even called "informalities." You must begin to realize that you're forever looking to increase your body strength and it's ALWAYS important and significant.

In order to feel your best you must take action to create some change. The majority of us just hope things will change, someday, someway, somehow. If you want them to change, YOU have to change them. No one else will do it for you. The fascinating part is that when you begin to take action, it will begin to appear as though others around you are beginning to help you. At first, the only resistance you'll have will be your own. Everything else will be easy.

I once explained this to a woman who was on over 15 medications and experiencing a great amount of stress in her life. We went through the concepts of Thought Shifting and controlling her thoughts and thinking. I broke down the three major areas that affected body energy and we started with meeting and greeting people. I said that when people asked how she was doing she should say, "GREAT!" She glared at me with total disbelief."What if I am NOT feeling great?" she asked. I replied, "Where do people typically ask you how are you?" She said, "Usually at work." I then inquired why she worked and she told me, "To make money." My follow-up question was, "And to do what?" She responded, "To do the things I enjoy doing." Then I asked, "When you do the things you enjoy, how do you feel?"She thought for a moment and said, "Well, I feel great!" flashing a wide smile. "Exactly!" I replied. "What makes you assume when they ask you how you are doing they are always asking about your worst problem?"As if a light bulb suddenly went off in her head, she quickly said, "The other person doesn't care how I feel," to which I explained, "Exactly. The answer is for YOU, not for them."

This wonderful woman has been a client of mine on and off for years, due to a variety of major personal and medical issues that have appeared in her life. Through all these issues, her new attitude and resulting inner strength has kept her balanced and helped her persevere. She is definitely doing GREAT.

Awareness – The 1st Key to Change

I cannot emphasize enough the importance of being aware of how you position yourself when saying the things that you say. You cannot be better than what you say. You don't want to say things that you don't want to come true. Always work towards what you want and desire through what you say. This wave of positive energy and intention will draw towards you those things you truly want to have happen. It is difficult to focus on the things you desire when you're focusing on negative thoughts and sayings. We are always talking and expressing something to others. You must remember to always project what you want into your imagined future. Any opportunities to make yourself feel better and to lift your body's energy needs to be recognized and used to keep you feeling as great as possible.

I want you to not only say positive things, but want you to realize they are true and how your body benefits from such a habit. The truth is your life is better than you realize, so it's time you realize it and start saying it. If you want to improve your life, you have to recognize how good it is before it'll get better. You will benefit at all levels of the body and mind, as will others with your positive energy around them.

A quick review to remember:

1. Always put your best forward, even if you feel like you've been limping! Answer the way you want to be. When asked for a response, at all times realize where you want to be and how great life really is. Your answer to "How are you?" should be, "GREAT!" or "Awesome!" or "Fantastic!" You cannot be better than what you say. So ALWAYS say where you want to be, NOT where you think you are.

2. Negative responses result in negative feelings, so always be aware of what you are saying and how it feels in the body.

3. If you don't want it to be true, DON'T SAY IT. The subconscious mind can't take a joke and takes things VERY literally. Little negative sayings you don't think mean anything, will mean EVERYTHING to your subconscious.

4. Never EVER say anything bad or negative about yourself, especially out loud to others. Never call yourself names or say you can't do something. Your subconscious mind will do EVERYTHING it can to make it all true. The subconscious mind will picture whatever you say and begin to attract it into your life.

"Happiness doesn't depend on any external conditions, it is governed by our mental attitude."
Dale Carnegie

Chapter Five

Negative Environment

How It Drains You By
Draining Your Body Energy

The next area we need to look at, review, and understand is how our environment plays a role in your feelings and body energy. If you surround yourself with negative things or people, you will have lower energy levels in your body, making you feel lethargic, weak, and drained. This will lower your immunity, open up your body to health problems, and take your focus off the fact that it's your environment causing these issues. Much like breathing in toxic fumes will make you sick, the dangerous energy from negative people that fills your eyes, ears, and other senses will also drain you.

Negative people or things that surround you will lead to negative thinking, negative self-talk, and negative conversations whenever you engage in communication with others. It may start somewhere else with someone in an innocent way, but you'll have a tendency to keep it going if you're unaware it is happening or what you need to do to stop it in its tracks.

Our new awareness will focus on negative externals, how to recognize them, minimize them, and in many cases, remove them entirely. This is something that's very important and most often overlooked; yet, it is also something that can be easily learned.

Negativity All Around Us

Dealing with negative people is something we need to be aware of every day. We'll learn to protect ourselves from the energy drain that takes place when in conversation with them. Negativity is very fascinating. As we begin to understand how it works, we'll be able to identify it and when we can't avoid it, we'll learn to neutralize it.

The key to keep in mind is that negative people give off a draining type of energy, which they need to do something with or pass along to someone else. It's like garbage you can't allow to accumulate. You must find a way to get rid of it.

We all know people who enjoy telling their negative situation or story to anyone who'll listen. Perhaps, it might even be something that you do. When these individuals speak about something negative, the end result is they suddenly feel better and the other person feels worse! It is as if they passed this huge weight off their shoulders and onto yours.

You must realize that anytime you feel worse after a conversation, you've been dumped on. That's right, you just made the other person feel better and now you feel drained of energy. This is a very dangerous situation because you open yourself up to the possibility of having others continually dump their issues on you.

Negative energy and water are quite similar, because they both flow evenly or downward. Water does not flow up a hill. Neither does negativity flow up towards positive people. It always flows downward.

The more your energy is lowered and reduced, the easier other negative people will find you and reuse you over and over. Have you become someone's dumping ground?

It's as if you become their toxic waste station. Once a pathway to you is created, it usually stays intact as a place for the negative person to continue ridding themselves of their negative energy and it's all on you!

The truth is they're not actually getting rid of the negativity. They're temporarily relieving some negative accumulation and then go get more because of their negative habits and behaviour. When their negative accumulation hits a certain level, they again look to whoever took it before. Unfortunately for you, it's as if accepting this garbage is your birth given responsibility in the name of friendship or a family connection. You will learn it is not.

Most likely, the individual doing the dumping doesn't know the cycle, which is the real sad part. It's like someone who has an infectious problem spreading it to those they spend the most time with. It might be friends and loved ones; in fact, the ones they would least want to hurt. We have a tendency to want to spend time with the people we love, like, or enjoy. Wouldn't it be great if we could unload the negativity on those we didn't like? It isn't that we can't, and I'm not advising to, it's just that we spend more time with people we are comfortable with and care about. The negativity of others often unknowingly seeps into us with such a steady stream that it never seems to end. Although done unintentionally by others, we will now begin to realize how tiring it really is to talk with certain loved ones or good friends.

Negativity Acts and Spreads Like A Disease

Negativity is a disease. Trust me, if the pharmaceutical industry could come up with a pill that eliminated negativity, you could bet your life they would have it labelled as a disease. A quick medical dictionary check for "disease" reveals the following: "Impairment of the normal state of the living animal or one of its parts that interrupts or modifies the performance of the vital functions and is a response to environmental factors." Negativity changes a person's body energy and weakens every part of it; including: organs, glands, and cells. If this isn't a disease, then what is? Just like a disease, it's also infectious.

By definition, an "infectious disease" is able to cause disease in other animals. Infectious pathologies are usually qualified as "contagious diseases" (also called communicable diseases), due to their potential of transmission from one person to another. That's what we're talking about! The spread of negativity is like an infectious, contagious disease. When you break it down, you'll see how bad negativity is and realize how necessary it is to work on identifying and eliminating it from your life. It's that vital to your survival. The unfortunate thing is that the majority of infected people are carriers, never knowing they are infected. They actually don't grasp how negative they really are. That's the sad truth, but it's also the most dangerous part. It's often those we trust and love to associate with the most that are the most infected. It can be a tricky balance, as some people don't have to be negative all the time to be a risk factor to be around.

Negativity Is So Accepted That Most Deny It Exists

Many people are negative, yet will deny it if asked. They're on this negative, cynical merry-go-round and have no clue how to get off. They may not even realize they're on it! Some are convinced that negativity is something that is actually their reality and their future. How sad and unfortunate is that thought?

No one knows what happened tomorrow or next week. Therefore, to look forward to an unknown future in a negative way not only breeds more negativity, it actually creates it. This is how powerful thinking and your thoughts really are. When you don't control your own thoughts, others around you will be controlling yours. This can also happen so unintentionally on their part. However, when you know it's happening, it's easier to change it. With a few simple rules and processes to follow, you can change everything.

When a person is continually negative, it becomes their habit, behaviour and belief. It has been proven that beliefs affect us down to the cellular level, because it has unfortunately become our reality. The truth is reality only exists inside your head. Knowing where it exists and knowing that you can change it are two different things. The most important thing is knowing HOW to change it and what to do.

Awareness is fundamental, as it opens up the realization of the issues and builds a desire to make it different, to change it. This is what you would think. Change is what you're looking for by reading this book. You are open minded enough to want to work new concepts and techniques into your thinking process. However, when you're not aware of others' negativity and what it's doing to you, it's like doing nothing for an illness that can be easily treated.

Many negative people I've helped identify areas they need to change often say, "It's reality and that's why I think and talk the way I do." But is it reality? If reality is all in your head, because it's your perception of what you consider is real or not real, then I choose to believe in a future of possibility and potential. I want that to be my reality and you should too. It's funny how when I changed those clients' perceptions of the future and taught them to control their "reality," their whole outlook changed.

I remember one client who was emotionally overwhelmed in all aspects of his life. He related how he was very stressed at the office, due to the constant friction and bad energy caused by his co-workers. We continued working on some of the processes with more awareness of what was going on with his thoughts and perceptions, versus what he really desired to have happen. During a conversation a few weeks later, I suddenly just asked him how work was going. His response was, "It seems as if everyone has changed."

When perceptions change and thoughts change, reality must change with it. Follow along with me for a bit here, it's going to get good!

Here's how it works: If a negative person talks to you, spreading their negative energy, perceptions, and reality, why does THAT now have to become YOUR reality? People are like ships aimlessly flowing in the direction of the last wind. How often has something you've heard or seen taken your mind to places you didn't want to go? For anyone untrained in the methods I'm teaching, the answer will be "much too often" or "all the time."

This no longer needs to be the case once I teach you what to do and how to do it. Again, awareness is the key. The first step is your connection to those people spreading their negativity and what you do in response during these situations.

You CAN Control Your Thoughts

We will next look at other areas of your environment that are taking your mind to places you don't need or want to be.

Are you as positive as you could be? Do you want 100% of all the thoughts in your head to come true? Do you find good things to say to those around you, especially those people you care about? If the answer is not 100% then yes, we need to fix it. If the individuals who surround you are negative and draining, we need to fix it. If you often find yourself in conversations with negative people, we need to fix it. We need to fix whatever it is that's draining you and making you feel something you weren't before being exposed to it. It could be anything or anyone. It really doesn't matter. Negativity has a way to find you, if you don't control your thoughts and thinking.

Look at all relationships. Who do you spend your time with? This includes physically and electronically. That's right, in our world of electronics we have phones, emails, texting, and computer chatting. Remember, anytime you interact with someone (in any form) and feel worse than when you started, you were basically dumped on.

Our goal is to identify the negative feelings and thoughts in your body and mind, then eliminate their causes and sources. When we can't eliminate them (i.e. a family member we might want to keep), we'll learn to limit the negativity and understand it differently. There will also be another very powerful intervention I will teach you, which I call "Spinning"(that will be fully explained later). It is designed to quickly get the other person off their current negative topic and onto another more positive one.

For now let's look at the first part of our awareness, which is how we're feeling. If you are uncomfortable, uneasy, anxious, etc., then quickly look at who you were interacting with (even if it wasn't face to face). You may begin to see a pattern of feeling a certain way only after associating with a particular group of people or individual.

Limiting Interaction With Negative People

If this is the case, we need to limit the interaction and the type of communication going on. We must limit the time we spend with such people or even go as far as to remove them from any regular interaction. I know there may be mixed emotions about doing this, and perhaps there are some people who can't be limited or removed. We will cover this, but please remember this is about your life and preserving the highest level of physical and mental health possible. It can't be taken lightly. I bet you already know who I'm talking about and can now see how their negativity affects you.

I tell clients this is why we have caller ID on our phones. It always surprises me when people run to answer a call, when it's often someone they'd rather not speak with at that moment. When you become convinced the negative person calling does not need your immediate attention, it might better prepare you to talk to them at your convenience, instead of theirs. If it's truly important, they'll call back or leave a message.

It's time to look at who you spend time with and the quality of these relationships. Is it benefiting you by making you feel more full of energy and full of life? Does it make you feel good when you walk away or hang up the phone? When you shut down the computer at night and head to bed, do you fall asleep peacefully or lay awake troubled about that last online conversation?

Keep in mind, it's all about how you feel when you walk away and things settle inside you. Weaning yourself off a negative relationship results in less exposure to the draining energy and damage this person has been inflicting on you. Remember, people have to unload their negativity, so in response you have to be on the lookout when it happens to you.

Relationships have to be examined. Where do you spend your time and with whom? These are hard questions to ask yourself. I am not suggesting you totally eliminate everyone from your immediate environment; however, there will be a few you'll need to limit time being around. People who don't make you feel good are not people with whom you need to associate. It doesn't mean that everyone always has to make you feel good. Yet, if they aren't making you feel at least as good as when you started interacting with them, we need to take some action.

After trying many therapies and therapists, one of my clients came to me very stressed. She just wasn't happy. She couldn't seem to put a finger on it. So we talked and talked about different things and on some occasions we talked about nothing. To clarify, it may have seemed like nothing to her but I was actually waiting to see where her subconscious was taking her. During one session, we began discussing her "single" status and the pressure she was feeling from her mother to have a grandchild. The poor woman didn't even have a man in her life and dear old mom was pressuring her to have a child! These weren't innocent suggestions or conversations, but real pressure she had to have a child because that's what her mother wanted.

After we identified and talked about the problem, on her own, my client began spending less time around her mom. The interesting result was she suddenly felt less pressure and stress in her life. She maintained a relationship with her mother; yet, made it more on her own terms, rather than her mother's. She also has a desire to be in a relationship with a partner, but without the pressure to have a child at this stage of her life (mid 40's).

Awareness and Honesty As To Who Is Causing Your Most Stress

We have to discover who is causing our unwanted stress and then make plans to change the situation, even if it's family. In fact, sometimes it is family that causes us the most grief and pressure. It is akin to thinking we are still a child and have to respond to the wishes and needs of siblings and parents. I suggest we have all due respect where it is deserved, but don't disrespect yourself when you now know what's happening with negative energy. Healthy relationships are important. Recognizing what is healhy and what is not is even more important.

The more you realize all this, the more you'll see it and that's a good thing. Of course, you can't get rid of everyone; although, at times that's what it feels like is needed. There are ways to get people to change what they're talking about and not to be so negative towards you. This is about controlling that negative energy. The average person doesn't control their thoughts or their thinking. If they did, they wouldn't be talking to you the way they do. They would realize that negativity also drains their energy. There are steps you can take when it does happen though.

The obvious solution is avoidance, where you limit the time you interact with the person. In severe negativity cases, you can completely limit your interaction and keep as much distance between the two of you as possible. This decision might only last until you feel strong enough to allow the person back into your life, albeit in smaller doses. There are also exceptions to every rule. Just because you don't feel good, doesn't necessarily mean it's the people in your environment; however, it's a good start. If you think about it, we're attracted to doing things with fun people who make us laugh and allow us to be ourselves. Then there are those who don't make us feel that way and we make excuses or decline their invitations. We already do this at a subconscious level. Now you can understand it both consciously and subconsciously, in order to make better choices and decisions in the future. It's these everyday choices and decisions that will determine how you feel. The nice thing is the choice will become more yours than someone else's.

You may find so much negativity swirling around your environment, that you won't be able to eliminate everyone! I don't suggest you do that anyway. I want you to become more fascinated and start to appreciate how you've been influenced for so long without realizing it.

Let's look at what to do when interacting with someone you've deemed "safe" to keep in your life, but who initiates a conversation in a negative way. As you'll recall from a previous section, it's very important what you say when starting off any new conversation. It's imperative to lead with the best introduction possible. Focus on the great and positive things in life. Never assume people can "see through" you and know anything about you at all. People not only cannot see through you, the truth is they really don't care. Everyone has their own issues and if they don't appear to, it's because the grass always seems greener on their side of the fence. Most people have some problem they're dealing with on a daily basis. If it isn't current, it's from their past and something they've never been able to get rid of on their own. Yes, even your "perfect" friends and neighbours have problems and issues.

You must remember that you're not obligated to tell anyone anything, if you don't want to do so. People who have had anything negative happen to them are constantly repeating the negative experience to others; thereby, only breeding more of the same. A client one time had a very traumatic experience occur to him and it was a newspaper feature. Of course, all his friends know how he almost lost his life in a boating accident due to another boater's negligence. After removing the traumatic event from his subconscious, I remember looking at him and saying, "Oh more thing - STOP telling the story!" He gave me this funny look and this stare, as he acknowledged that every place he went people would ask him to repeat what had happened to him. Every time he repeated the story, he regressed back with full emotions to that terrorizing scene. I removed that terrible emotion; nevertheless, I told him there was no longer any reason to retell the tale, nor was he obligated to repeat it ever again. If you have a bad story, STOP REPEATING IT!

You are going to realize that 99.99% of the general population has no idea how to control their thinking. This problem is then compounded when these same people start controlling your thoughts! They do this by initiating conversations in a negative manner. They focus on their own worst problems and then invite you to add more fuel to their fire of personal despair. The spiral begins and feeds itself a self-supporting diet of negative energy. This is happening right now and has for a long, long time.

Being aware of the cycle will allow you to take preventative measures and inoculate yourself against this infectious process. I believe one of the most interesting aspects of becoming aware is realizing what was happening to you in the past. Based on all the negativity from your environment, you'll begin to grasp why you've been feeling the way you have been. Once you understand this concept, you can take a step back and understand it in ways that will now allow you to change it.

Let's briefly return to the example of dealing with a "safe" person, who periodically gets caught up in something bad and throws it towards the first person who will listen. Remember, the person doing this doesn't realize what's going on and we need to intervene, to shift them into a different thought pattern. So here's the scene: A friend states a negative comment to you and starts going off about it, looking for you to join in or agree how bad things really are. Here's a great way to quickly stop it. Simply ask them, "What are you doing about it?" If they respond that they're doing nothing, simply tell them: "Then don't complain. What else is going on?" This exchange will allow you to continue the conversation in a different direction. If, however, they respond with a plan or something proactive, reply: "Great! Then it should be better soon. What else is going on?" Then take the conversation to a better place.

Again remember, your friend had no control over their thinking and had no idea what was really going on. If they did, would they be saying those things to you? Things that suck the very life force out of you and of themselves? I think not! Using the above examples will help both you and others, as the change in direction happens so fast. You'll actually be training them to change their thoughts and what they say around you, and more and more when they're with others. One of my favourite ways to do this is a process that I call "Spinning."

*"Most people do not control their thoughts
so do not let them control yours"*
Rick Saruna

Chapter Six

Spinning:

How to Quickly Change the Direction on Someone's Negativity

In this process, I will explain how to quickly get a person off a topic and into a different direction. It might be because they're talking in a negative way or maybe even making you uncomfortable in some manner. It happens more than you think and when you become aware, you may notice it happens quite a bit.

Oh, before I forget, I just wanted to ask you to do a quick memory test! Okay? Here it goes: What color is your front door? What was your favourite grade in high school? And finally, what was your favourite movie that you've watched in the past few months?

Great, thank you!

Now what were we talking about before all that nonsense? You see, I just told you about changing the subject quickly and easily and then I did it, without most even realizing it.

Spinning is about making something sound important by changing your tone, increasing the volume, or sound in a hurry, etc. When applying this, I watch for a person to look away when thinking of my question. It's as if they are searching in their mind for the answer. That is one spin. Then when they come back to my eyes, I ask another question, until they look away again. Spin two! They will then come back to look at me; now, I ask my third question, causing yet another look away. Spin three! By then they're so confused, you simply say: "So what else is going on?" or "I have to go. It was great talking! See ya!"

It is important to continually guide them during the spin, letting them "search" for the answer, coming back to you with their eyes, and then asking something else somewhat related to the last question. Three good spins and you will be in the clear. If they don't look away, you MUST ask a question that gets them to THINK and try to remember something, even if it's complete nonsense.

The key is making the first spin sound important and then they will follow!

Happy Spinning!

External influences on how we feel and think are huge. We have yet to mention or cover another area even more significant than the people around you. Those individuals in your environment are very important, because friends, family, work, and routines enable us to mingle constantly with people. Thus, throughout the day we are connecting with others, sending and receiving some sort of energy, suggestions, ideas, and influences. Consequently, this connecting could just be unloading a mega dose of negative garbage onto you!

If that in itself isn't enough to digest, there's something else we need to spend time on. There is one area that can be more negative and energy reducing than what we've already discussed. As hard as that might be to believe, we must also be aware of other environmental sources of negativity. The key to remember is that anything you let inside your mind influences your thoughts, your thinking, and your emotions. Anything that has such power over you needs to be examined closely.

"*The media's the most powerful entity on earth. They have the power to make the innocent guilty and to make the guilty innocent, and that's power. Because they control the minds of the masses.*"

Malcom X

Chapter Seven

The News, Media, and Other Mind Altering Processes

An area I've discovered that can quickly change the direction of the masses in a severe negative way is that of the media. One might be surprised how such a group, that we believe have our best interest at heart, could do such a harmful thing. I'm talking about the information fed to us and accepted as whole-heartily as the truth. I'm talking about the news and the big headlines, all the way down to the local interest stories. I'm talking about some of the most negative thoughts and energy we are exposed to day after day, through all the forms of news media. Regrettably, most people accept these stories with little, if any, filter of disbelief.

One of the first things I do for a client dealing with any stress or anxiety is to put them on a "news fast." What is a news fast? It's exactly how it sounds: the elimination of the news from your environment. I mean ALL news. That means the TV, the newspapers, the radio, and the internet (not email and chatting or searching - only if it's anything negative from any news source.) It also includes anything else where you read, see, or hear about people, activities, and events that create a negative reaction in your body and mind.

Let's look at this in order to better appreciate the importance of filtering what you allow into yourself. One of the most profound things I've discovered about myself is that I can actually control my thinking. If I can control my thinking and my thoughts, so can you. It wasn't always this way. Not until I discovered how to do it and how to teach it to others. When a client discovers this, there's an immediate shift in awareness and consciousness. There is an awakening, which like anything else, no one can make you experience it, nor can you make someone else realize it unless they are willing. Just as with your willingness to change, this awareness is a reflection of your desire to shift emotional experiences from one of the unpredictable, to one of certainty and direction. You may not even know the direction you desire to go. However, you do know you don't like the direction you've been going in and that you can be doing better. We usually don't look for change, unless something has created a situation that results in some chaos or confusion in our lives. Confusion is a learning state that always comes before opportunity. Most people who become confused miss the opportunity to take inventory, and then change the direction of their lives. That's why this is all about awareness, then recognizing the opportunity to implement the techniques, and finally, watching change happen automatically; in many cases, quickly. It's the use of these techniques and methods over time that'll create a long-term shift and change of a lifetime.

The difficulty in thinking differently is that with so much information bombarding on us, we don't have time to think. The other problem is it's often those we trust the most who attack the hardest. People have a tendency of trusting news reports and feeling that the daily news reporter is our trusted friend. Then they remove all filters of disbelief and absorb all the news as 100% total truth, which is never the case.

Just Trying To Get Through Each Day

For many, the stress is so high that people simply want to make it through the day. They just want to get by, get through, and survive. At times, it's a cruel world out there and it's hard enough feeling safe and comfortable, let alone confident enough to achieve your goals. This is why we need to control what we allow into the private inner world of our mind.

How rough is it really out there? A short time ago, I met with a man in his 30s for some anxiety work. He had a gloomy attitude towards life and the future. A terrible situation to be in would be an understatement. One of the interesting aspects about this individual was he lived in a tranquil community in southern Ontario. I have visited this area many times and know that it's a very nice, quiet, and safe place. During our initial conversation, I said he needed to start looking forward to a future of unlimited possibilities, which might include seeing himself getting married, and perhaps one day having children.

"Children?" he snapped back at me. "Not in a world like this!"

Not in a world like this? What is this guy thinking? He lives in a beautiful, quaint town on the shores of one of the Great Lakes. It made me realize that our perceptions were quite different. I asked him about the "a world like this?" comment and immediately knew his picture of the world was not the world he actually lived in. Instead, it was the world presented to him by others, but who was tainting his perceptions?

He explained he lived with his parents out of convenience, not of necessity. He considered himself quite independent; although, he did spend a bit of time with his parents. I knew his world view was being influenced by someone or something, but probably both. I asked, "Do you watch a lot of news?" to which he almost snapped back, "Well, yes! My dad says we need to watch the news to know what's going on in the world." That certainly answered many questions! It was more than obvious why he was scared, anxious, and fearful. Every morning this poor young man woke up to the worst stories of the night. All the tragedies of the world were presented to him, which happened while he was sleeping (or tying to sleep). All we have to do to understand his perceptions of "his" world as he knew it would be to follow him around for a day. Only then would we know what he was experiencing and understand how he wasn't controlling his thinking. This happens to everybody. Our environment and the information we get from it becomes the reality we try to live in day after day.

Our Reality Is Only What We Think It Is

Another area that's overlooked as a major influence in thoughts and emotions is the media, news, and television programming. Today's news is not journalism; it's sensationalism. It's all about ratings and rankings. The news also has a take no prisoners attitude. The more intense and emotional the reporting becomes, the higher the ratings. News is about showing the most intense emotional stories available, no matter where they've happened.

In the past, it often took days for news stories from certain regions of the world to reach us. Now, we are instantaneously watching as it happens. People witness the news unfold right before their eyes. Millions of people watched the tragedy of September 11th in real time. Eyewitnesses to doom and gloom, provided by the networks. This was unheard of years ago. Not today. The quicker they can get to some hot spot to give you close ups of those suffering, the higher their ratings.

Several years ago, the low-speed car chase involving a famous ex-football player was viewed by people via a news helicopter's camera, as it tracked the incident wind down the highways of California. News can now be presented like an action adventure movie, filled with emotion and play-by-play commentary. Everything the journalists say and do will take you on a mental journey, where you might not want to go. It is like a roller coaster ride, which you don't know where the next twist or turn will be or if the ride will ever end.

It's about building a news story filled with "the emotion of the moment" and if this isn't present, it's now about creating it. All media seems to operate the same. Work the viewer's emotional state and then leave them hanging as long as you can. Is this reporting? Is this passing along useful information? What exactly is it? That might be the best question, but I know what it is to me: it's something I don't like. It doesn't make me feel good and it takes me places I don't want to be.

It's not that I can't face the truth. On the contrary, I do want the truth. I want it unbiased, with both sides of the story given to me. Not the opinions of someone competing with a movie director for sensationalism. I often wonder if the people in charge of media outlets really understand what they're trying to achieve or what they're actually doing to the general population. They attempt to be unbiased, but it often doesn't turn out that way, does it? Sometimes they run an incomplete story because it's more of a race between networks than an honest attempt to make sure they tell you what's really going on. Do they even worry about the truth?

Anything on television is about one thing: ratings. It isn't about the truth, it isn't about you; it's about the network and their ratings.

The worse thing about this is some people base their lives on the news. It's a sad fact. We all know someone who is always talking about what they saw on the news or happily spreading the latest gossip. They can recite word for word from paper or magazine articles. Sometimes you've read the same story and when you begin to talk to these individuals on the subject, you realize they're quoting from it! These people then base their lives all around the news, forming opinions and thoughts from the reports they see and hear. This is the case with print, radio, and television media. Television is scripted to present a certain angle to a story. They show pictures, they do interviews, and present experts to support the views of the station. You really don't have time to think or process any of it. It is so well written and flowing, it's like you're heading downstream on a raft without a paddle. There isn't much you can do. Next thing you know, another story flashed on the screen before you can figure out what happened with the last one. It goes on and on.

Where Do Most Get Their Information?

I recently researched some statistics that are both astounding and frightening. A 2003 research study showed the following data:

- ➢ Most people get their information from TV.
- ➢ Fewer than 15% of people actually read books.
- ➢ 1/3 of high school graduates never read another book for the rest of their lives.
- ➢ 42 % of college graduates never read another book after college.

➢ 80 % of U.S. families did not buy or read a book last year.

➢ 70 % of U.S. adults have not been in a bookstore in the last five years.

➢ 57 % of new books are not read to completion.

Each day in the United States, people spend four hours watching TV, three hours listening to the radio, fourteen minutes reading magazines, and how much more time on the world wide web? It is constantly increasing with the internet now available everywhere, via wireless hotspots or data plans. It's on your desktop, laptop, phone, and media players. You can read the news, emails, and texts wherever you're standing. You don't have to think anymore. In fact, in today's world thinking appears to be highly discouraged. If you think, you might realize the things you're seeing, hearing, and feeling are making you uncomfortable and you need to turn them off! That's why thinking is no longer encouraged. Some of you might remember television announcers saying, "Don't touch that dial!" as a warning not to turn their program off during the commercial break. People would actually listen and not touch the dial. It's funny how TV can control a person's perception of reality and become their reality of the truth.

Once again, if you don't control what goes in, you will have problems with what's going on inside. Once you control what you let in, it'll become easier to control what's going on inside the place that is your reality.

What Is True or Not True?

I saw an amusing web segment once showing a video titled, "It Must Be True Because I Saw It on the Internet!" How funny is that? It was making light of the fact that so many people think that if they see it on the news or the internet, it must be true. Many people will deem news and internet knowledge as truth, which they then absorb and use as a basis for their own thoughts and as a point of reference. How much further from the truth could this basis actually be?

Weekly tabloids are the worst with their outrageous headlines and outright fabricated stories. A classic example: "Lonely UFO Aliens Are Stealing Our Pets" (*National Examiner* - 9/6/88). In the early days, *National Enquirer* staffers were infamous for fabricating incredible stories to create sales enticing headlines, attracting customers who still held the naïve belief that "they couldn't print it if it wasn't true."

Remember why the media does any of this: to increase readership, which in turn increases their worth to advertisers. It isn't because they simply want to deliver information and news; it's to find the information and news that'll attract people. They don't care how they do it. Just look at the paparazzi. If there wasn't a demand for sensationalism, these people wouldn't exist. Over the years, news organizations worked hard to increase their readers' emotional responses to their already highly emotional stories. No one wants to be outdone, so when one network goes above and beyond, the other networks soon follow suit. They don't care how you respond, as long as you keep coming back and talking about them to others. It's all about their readership and audience, nothing more.

If it was about "you" then maybe these organizations would realize some of the topics they've been talking about are harmful. Perhaps they would want to make sure they put you into a good mood and make you feel better about yourself, or the future of your children. If they really cared, would they continue to sneak around invading people's privacy and threatening their safety to get pictures and videos of them? You would hope they'd respect victims of horrific accidents and not plaster them all over the news for the world, under the guise of an "Exclusive!"

No one is safe from the "excuse" called news. Their stories, their interviews, and their one-sided slants to increase ratings make nothing sacred.

On the other hand, there are those who will say, "But it's reality." Yes, it is. The reality THEY decided to create and show you. It's not your decision to feature THAT story. You don't have a say in what you're going to see; especially, in how it will make you feel.

Let's look at something. Do you tell your children everything? I mean *everything*? The bills, the relationship with your spouse? Do you let your children watch horror movies and unrated programs? I would have to say I most certainly hope you don't. Why don't you? Do they need to know the "reality" of everything? Of course not. We protect them. We want them to be stress free and enjoy life, right? Well, when does that change for you? When are you supposed to "grow up" and take on the perils of the world? I also want to know how witnessing plane crashes or victims of car crashes are going to help you become a better person? I want to know how watching fires and hearing about how people passed away needlessly are going to make you sleep better tonight?

I'm not saying these issues aren't important, as it might motivate certain people to help others or to do public service, donating their time or money. It would be different if they showed us how to prevent these things from happening instead of focusing on the trauma and the tragedy. Unfortunately, this is not the case in most situations. Instead, it stresses people out, causing fear and worry. If you were to examine what kinds of stories are printed or broadcasted each day, you'd be surprised to see how the media can put a negative twist into almost anything.

So, tell me, where are all the feel good, heart-warming reports of caring people doing great things and sacrificing their time and money to help others in need? The stories that make you feel warm and fuzzy, restoring your faith in the human race, as well as the sense that you can make a difference too. When is the last time you read the paper or watched the news and afterwards could honestly say it made you feel happy to be alive? Not very often and definitely not often enough.

Happy News Is Hard To Come By

Negative news isn't the sort of thing you'd want a stressed person watching, is it? Would you take an anxious person to watch a horror movie? Would you take a water phobic person to see *The Titanic* film? I don't think so. This is why it's of utmost importance to shield yourself and loved ones from things that won't improve the quality of their lives and their thoughts. By now, I trust you are realizing that the quality of a person's thoughts is in direct correlation to the quality of their lives.

Thoughts are the quality of life. No one has ever been happy with sad thoughts. No one. It isn't possible. The way to feel happy is to fill your mind with thoughts of happiness. Remember the happy times, the fun things, the great people, and the amazing experiences. These are the thoughts that will put smiles on faces and joy into lives. Now tell me, does the news do this to you?

News is like drinking alcohol. Some experts say that a drink here and there can be healthy, especially wine. In small amounts it's said to be good; but if you drank several bottles a day, you'd have a problem, right? Well, the news is like that with most people not only "buzzing," but intoxicated on the cheapest booze available. Think of the headache the next day! To me, that's the essence of the news, and the best way not to let it affect your mind and body is to eliminate it from your environment. Unfortunately for many individuals, the news is so stimulating they can't stop taking it in. They become news junkies. These same people then arrive at my office and admit they are news addicts. They tell me their thoughts are negative, or they have trouble sleeping, or that stress is overwhelming, as are their anxiety levels. Do you think anyone with these symptoms is controlling their inner voice? Not likely.

I often talk about how people want to know the following day's weather forecast; so before they go to sleep, they watch the late newscast while waiting for the weather segment. They then wonder why they experience troubled sleep and disturbing dreams. In the morning, they wake up to a cup of coffee and get more news from their paper, radio, or internet. Next, they jump in their cars for their commute to work and listen to talk radio. It's not surprising that by the time they reach the office, they feel like they're having a bad day! Looking back over the past 8-10 hours, at no point were they controlling their thinking. Thoughts control your thinking, your feelings, and emotional responses. They are not as random as you think or have been led to believe. Anything you see, hear, or experience will and does have an effect you.

Clients come to see me because they need control over how they feel. When you change your thoughts, your thinking changes, and you begin to take control. This is when everything transforms and the fun begins. True joy will enter your life as you begin to take these principles and use them in your life.

"The primary cause of unhappiness is never the situation but thought about it. Separate them from the situation … It is as it is."
Eckhart Tolle

Chapter Eight

Thoughts Are Too Important To Be Left To Chance

Thoughts have been left to random chance for too long. It creates a reality that's often the reality of everything else around us and not something we'd ever crave. Feeling stressed is an obstacle to achieving the goals we truly desire. We want to be in control of our thoughts and our thinking. You don't even have to feel out of control to benefit from any of this advice. If you want to feel better and maintain good health, follow some of these simple processes. As we've discussed, the most important process is to become aware of your environment. Since the news is something people have a tendency of unquestionably believing, it bypasses many filters that would normally be applied. It's almost immediately and totally absorbed into the subconscious. This is why viewers watch the same newscasters regularly, because they've "let them in" and trust them. However, there are no filters, which results in the broadcasted information being sent directly to our subconscious as truthfulness. This is NOT a good thing.

Remember, the news has an agenda and it doesn't include your health or well-being. They even speak with a "forked tongue" saying one thing and then doing the opposite. When I was getting the local paper, I enjoyed solidifying my position on its negativity by isolating the downbeat articles (only reading the headlines) and wondering just how many people read every word of these stories. One day was especially interesting; I might say it was funny, except it was really more on the sad side than anything. Sad, because it was an irony beyond all measures.

The community was hit hard by an economic downturn and the paper was more negative than a worker on indefinite layoff. It was absolutely terrible. Every story was pessimistic about the city's financial woes; yet on this morning, I found a "Letter from the Editor" wrapped on the outside of the paper (I guess it couldn't wait for the editorial pages). In his heartfelt letter addressed to "The People of the Community," the Editor spoke about how the city was getting a "bad rap" and everyone needed to be more positive and upbeat. He went line after enthusiastic line about how proud he was of "our city" and "our community," etc., encouraging the residents to please stop saying negative things about the city.

Now for the kicker: When you took that sheet off the front page of the paper, there for the entire community to see were all those negative, condemning headlines about the city! Obviously, the editor wasn't reading his own paper! It was beyond ridiculous and hypocritical for him to preach one message in his letter, only to put forward the exact opposite message on the front page.

Now it might seem like I'm really putting it to the paper, but that's just one form of media. There are so many more.

Let's take radio talk shows as another example. Instead of playing relaxing music in the morning, many stations have morning DJs. Most mornings you'll find a host saying something about someone and it isn't always very pleasant. I find listening to the radio especially important to monitor because people go into "road trance" while driving. How many times have you driven from work or from an errand, got home and wondered how you actually got there, forgetting the entire ride? It happens all the time. It's a hypnotic trance state. In hypnosis, the subconscious mind opens up to absorb words, thoughts, ideas, and suggestions. The radio "shock jock" is not the one you want to be hypnotizing you in the mornings! Or anytime, for that matter. People need to monitor what they listen to, watch, or read. This includes night-time TV, as you often fall asleep during the program. I tell everyone to turn off the volume, if they need to leave the TV on to fall asleep. The reason is that as you're falling off to sleep and in a light sleep state, you'll absorb the commercials and wake up wanting a hamburger or whatever other latest thing they are trying to sell you!

The brain has a filter to stop you from accepting everything said to you as truth. If someone on the street makes a statement you don't like, you usually don't absorb it.

You may not like what was said, but you would easily disagree with them and walk away.

The news stations are quite versed in behaviours and habits of people. We trust familiarity. We trust friends. We trust certain news reporters because we believe we almost actually know them. We see them everyday at the same time. In the "old" days, the news station reporters never spoke to each other or "mingled" on the air. Now they talk amongst themselves and we're drawn into their personalities. Subsequently, the more we get to "know" them, the more they become "friends."

With the filter down, we then absorb what's said and what they show us more deeply, which has the potential to cause us harm. When this happens, we're not controlling our thinking. Instead, someone else is controlling our thoughts and our thinking; therefore, also controlling our emotional responses. Not a good thing, especially when the stories are even worse.

The internet is also now a very powerful tool that delivers various forms of media to us. People will read their newspaper or different papers on the internet. The Net has given so much power to the masses, by being an immediate source of knowledge and information. Information is often called power and rightfully so. The power comes through education and knowledge. It is at everyone's fingertips with an internet connection. Now, one would think that having this information so close at hand would create a paradigm shift and take everyone to another level, right? Yes, it has that potential; yet, there are still a few problems with this.

As you know, when you do a computer search, thousands of entries come up based on what you were looking for at the time. The problem arises from negative thinking people looking for things in the only way they know how: negatively! This, of course, only solidifies and creates more negativity. I see this all the time in my clinic. A person with a health issue goes online, finds a website listing their symptoms, searches all the worst case scenarios, bookmarks the site, copies down the information, and finally, reads it over again and now remembers the information as fact!

The Mind Learns Through Things Repeated

The mind learns through spaced repetition. What is repeated is learned and absorbed. What you surround yourself with will affect you at all levels of the body and mind. I tell people with health issues to stop looking up symptoms and reading all those posts of negative people who don't believe they'll ever get better. That's not the environment or attitude that'll get you better. When you want to get better, you need to cleanse and purify your environment. This includes everything read, listened to, and watched through all forms of media, as well as anything that you allow to enter your mind. Yes, what YOU allow. Now that you're aware of this, it'll become your responsibility to follow it through.

A man in his mid-50s came to me with an issue he'd suffered from on a daily basis for over 40 years. He was a highly successful, educated business executive, whose wife I was able to help five years earlier. He researched a rare and peculiar problem (or so he thought) and soon found a doctor who had a following of other people with the same affliction! This doctor had a fancy name for the problem, but he might as well have placed stickers on his clients' foreheads, as he labelled them all with this issue. For years, the doctor supposedly worked diligently trying to free them from it. My client dutifully followed along, taking this learned man's advice and listening to the others' plights and emotional distress. He read endless heartbreaking stories of how difficult it was to function with such an issue and discovered he could only hope for slight improvements here and there. However, from my standpoint, more troubling was the fact he felt acknowledged by this group of suffers, connected to them. The "We're all in this together," mentality.

Through my applied process of emotional release for the locked-in emotion, followed by using the Thought Shifting process, this difficult issue seemed to magically vanish in a matter of weeks. Not only did it disappear, we began laughing about it. My client told me, "I can't believe everyone in that group is continuing to suffer in their reinforced stories of endless pain, with no end in sight." He'd realized that as comforting as it was to connect with others, it only made him think there was no way to alter his situation. Through Thought Shifting, his situation was easier to change when we modified his thoughts and thinking.

Always looking for what you want and need is critical when trying to create the life you desire, no matter what emotional situation in which you find yourself. It is vital to seek what you desire, not what others are talking about or thinking. Your transformation begins with the self-acknowledgement that no matter how "insignificant" or "crazy" others might believe your motive for change is, the sole reason is real to you. You have to accept and realize this first, in order to start working on doing something about it.

We have two little dogs that we are crazy about and it's easy for me to talk to anyone about their pets and pet stories. One time, I was ordering takeout food and the conversation went to the order taker's pet dog; a breed often plagued with certain health issues, as well as known for a shorter lifespan than many other types. This individual immediately mentioned his dog was getting up near that age. I asked, "What is the oldest recorded age of your dog's breed?" but he didn't know. I said he should find out and then ask himself, "Why couldn't my dog live as long or close to the oldest one?" You see, all the internet research he was doing only dealt with health problems and issues. This might be great preventative information for some, but positive people enjoy those moments of health anyway and expect to have them in the future. By the way, the dog we had before our current two lived for 19 and a half years – yes, 19.5 human years!

Getting back to the negative impact of the media and its various forms, it's not just the news, it also includes casual reading, TV programming, and movies. I once told a stressed middle-aged woman to go on a news fast and she replied, "That will be no problem because I love to read." I thought that was great but I knew by her negativity levels something else was still going on. I asked what she liked to read and she joyfully responded, "Murder mysteries!"I said, "You mean someone is dead and we don't know who killed them?" and I smiled a slight grin at her. With a half laugh, she agreed as I said, "No," to her and the negative stories. This also includes sad, scary movies and programming.

Years ago, when my two kids were in high school, they wanting to know if we could all go the show. I said, "Sure, what do you want to see?" They responded something that to me meant "blah, blah, blah," as I had no idea what the movie was about. So I asked, "How's this movie going to make me feel?" to which my son replied, "It's a scary movie." I quickly made up my mind and told them, "Sorry, but I'm not going." My son challenged, "Why, you don't want to be scared?" and broke out in laughter. I remember saying back to him, "I don't want to be scared because all week long people pay me to get rid of their fears and I'll be darned if I pay someone to scare me!"

I don't know about you, but it isn't uncommon for me to be thinking about a movie I saw in a theatre or watched on TV for days on end; thus, they really do have an effect! It all makes a difference. We can never be too careful about controlling what media we're exposed to on a daily basis. If you don't control it, it will control you.

Control the Media You Watch

Does this mean you can never watch the news or a sad show or movie? Of course not. This is about awareness. Your awareness to your environment and how it makes you feel. When you aren't feeling good, I want you to pay attention to the environment. Just stop for a second and become totally aware of YOUR personal environment. This includes the things you interact with, the people you talk to, and everything in between that you've been letting into your world. Everything that you let into your world enters into your head and into your subconscious mind. It should be by invitation only; otherwise, you risk less than desirable guests showing up and forcing you to concentrate on unwanted topics that then play in your thoughts. These unwelcome thoughts can play over and over in your mind, like that annoying song you just can't seem to shake.

So, if you're feeling "off" and something doesn't feel right or you catch yourself thinking less than positive thoughts, stop and ask yourself, "What am I thinking of? What just happened? Who was I talking to? What did I just read?" It could be something playing in the background, people talking, maybe the TV, or even the radio that you thought you weren't listening to, but subconsciously you were.

The nice benefit about these techniques is that as you begin implementing them into your day-to-day life, you'll become more sensitive to shifts in your thoughts, feelings, and body sensations. That's a good thing! This will allow you to make the changes to create the shift in your thoughts.

Awareness is the key, the tools will set you free, and the prevention techniques will make it easier each day.

This reminds me of a story. Some years ago, I was driving to the office when a feeling of tension and anxiousness unexpectedly came over me, entering my relatively calm body. Thankfully, I have a technique I use for this type of situation that we'll discuss later. Unfortunately, many people have no idea how to stop these negative feelings in their tracks. (Fortunately, we'll soon be learning how in the section dealing with "the inner voice.")

The first thing I did was to become thoroughly aware of my present situation and asked myself all of the aforementioned questions. The last thing I do is focus on the problem. Think about that. The last thing I do is to focus on the problem or the sensation in the body. The sensation is the warning sign to pay attention, not to refocus your attention and energy on the unwanted sensation. Remember, you cannot NOT think of something. If I tell you not to think of a blue tree right now, you must think of one. You can think you are not, but all you did was cover up the blue tree with something else.

I once told a client that it's impossible to process a negative, which I demonstrated to her. I said, "Whatever you do, do not think of a pink elephant right now." Most people just smile and you know that's what they're thinking about. Instead, this lady just stared blankly at me and you could see the focus in her head. I asked her what she was thinking of and she told me, "A brown cow." Interesting, I thought. So I asked her to do me a favour and move the brown cow aside and tell me what was behind it. Her face immediately relaxed, as she smiled and said, "There is a pink elephant."

So, getting back to my troubling drive to work tale. Once I believed that this uncomfortable feeling was a symptom and not the actual issue, I became aware of my thoughts, as well as any environmental inputs. I realized the radio was playing in the background and during the news segment the announcer had stated, "There was a school bus crash this afternoon." I instantly realized I was thinking of my own school-aged children in a bus crash. I was feeling uneasy, anxious, and worried. Then I remembered that my kids didn't ride the bus to school and the story happened 100 miles away! It didn't matter, because we always place ourselves in the first person when listening to, reading, or watching any story. Even though it was in the background and not in my "thought processes," it had absolutely affected me and it was absorbed immediately. If I didn't know what I've learned, I'd surely think my symptoms were an issue of unknown origin; that in itself would perpetuate even more anxious thoughts and feelings! The seeds of anxiety are long forgotten, as the issue becomes the symptoms and physical responses rather the actual original cause. Anxiousness in itself causes its own self perpetuating anxiety.

You Can't Cure Negative Feelings Without Knowing Their Cause

If you don't work on the initial issue, the underlying problem never goes away. You are simply "painting over it."

Most emotional "paint jobs" are poor, spotty, and don't cover up enough to completely change your thinking. So when a stressful thought comes up, no matter from where or how, the faster you become aware of it, the sooner you can deal with the root cause and not just the symptoms of the body sensations. The reaction gets your attention, but it's finding and dealing with the root cause that'll get you the cure. What people always focus on are the symptoms, which take on a life of their own. This isn't to say that the symptoms aren't serious or severe and I'd never suggest that they aren't even real. They are REAL. If you are thinking something, it becomes your reality. But remember, reality only exists within your own head.

Peripheral Attention and Peripheral Absorption

If you give anything your attention, it becomes a thought and then your reality. This attention to these thoughts does not have to be intentional. It can be peripheral attention and peripheral absorption. I take this from the term "peripheral vision." For those who don't know what that means, let me explain. Peripheral vision is if you stare straight ahead at this page, you will still notice things off the page in your environment (i.e. a table, a bookcase, a plant), but you aren't consciously thinking about these things. It's a survival thing really. If something appears as a threat, no matter what else you're doing, you need to pay attention to it. Like an animal in the wild, if they don't pay attention to what is going on around them, they may not get a second chance.

As you read this page, if something moves in your peripheral view, you will pay attention to it. That's an instinct. We are hardwired to it. By understanding this though, we can work with it and our emotional responses. Our goal is to work on the causes more and with the symptoms less. The more quickly we are aware of the initial causes, the symptoms will lessen and you'll begin to feel a sense of control and calmness that you may have never felt. The real problem is the way we're hardwired, from the biological side the response is "fight or flight." Either we physically confront the problem or we run for the hills. This is not possible in today's society. Well, it is a possibility, but it's not functional nor legal to punch someone! The whole idea of rules and regulations is to eliminate our natural reaction to "fight or flight." The issue is that most are "thinking" or processing in a negative way that things will not work out. Many of our issues are perceptions brought on by peripheral absorption without realizing it is happening. This so-called innocent background activity is like the power of a subliminal message. A subliminal message is something that's intentionally delivered to you, without you realizing it. These messages are not only absorbed by the subconscious, they're played out in a multiple of situations and endings, depending on your overall attitude and past points of reference. People, who have become negative due to an overexposure of worry and negative thinking, develop an expectancy of failure and will actually feel the effects of failure before an event occurs! This in turn will not only guarantee negative feelings, but will surely attract the failure as a subconscious goal. As you recall from previous pages, the mind cannot process a negative. Negative thoughts will attract negative feelings; subconsciously, the mind will attempt to give you what you focus on, positive or negative.

The subconscious is a multi-tasking super computer. It is capable of doing incredible things. It controls your breathing, your heart rate, your digestion, the cellular division of millions and millions of cells each second, and so many other amazing tasks, all at exactly the same time. This also includes making you feel the way you feel for a variety of reasons and situations. It is the misunderstanding of your reaction to these situations that creates stress, strain, confusion, and in many cases health issues. Instead of looking for the causes, we run to the symptoms.

The need to quickly control any thoughts that "sneak" into your mind cannot be overstated. This whole process of changing your thoughts and thinking by Thought Shifting is all about controlling your emotional response. Many people want to improve their lives for two reasons: to gain pleasure or to avoid pain. I don't believe that anyone knows what pleasure is, if they've never felt pain. The key is to control the pains and empower the pleasurable parts of life. You need to be aware of what's going on, in order to change it. Focus on the cause, not the symptom.

Always Focus On The Cause to Remove The Symptoms

I remember helping a client with severe anxiety some years ago. We started to work on changing her thoughts and her thinking; within a couple of weeks, everything appeared to be going very well. However, one day she came in and said she'd felt some anxiety the previous afternoon. I inquired, "On a scale of 0 to 10, how bad was the anxiety?" to which she replied, "About a 6, I guess." I questioned, "Like your mind was racing 60 miles an hour?" She exclaimed, "Yes! Exactly!" I explained to her, "The interesting thing is that if you are at zero, you don't just suddenly go to 60. You first have to pass 10, then 20, then 30, then 40, then 50, before you reach 60. You have to recognize the reactions and the feelings before they reach a point where the symptoms are scarier than the thoughts. The lower the number, the easier any change will be to implement. Being aware of your body and using our techniques will allow you to quickly make some of the changes."

In the case of anxiety, when the symptoms start showing up, it perpetuates itself and people then become anxious about being anxious! We also have a Thought Shifting program specifically for these individuals, because that's how bad the problem has become. It really can be an easy fix for most anxiety sufferers.

True awareness is a combination of being attentive to the increase in the changes and "levels" inside your body, as well as what's happening in your environment that could be causing it. If you find this difficult to do, it's not because you can't; it's that you're not used to consciously figuring out the subtle changes that are giving you clues to pay attention. Remember to always focus on any changes in the right direction and give yourself credit for even the slightest positive corrections. It becomes easier once you realize you can do it, learn the steps to implement these changes, and practice them.

One of the easiest ways to apply change is to realize how other things affect the way we think; therefore, the way we feel. At this point, we'll work on eliminating some obvious and not so obvious areas of concern. What we allow into us will radiate within us. If you want to create change, you'll have to change a few things. This is vitally important to your happiness and stress reduction. I want you to take nothing for granted and leave nothing to chance. Everything around you will affect you. Even if you've been doing something for years and think it's never had a negative effect on you, it's important to leave no stones uncovered.

Eliminating the obvious stressors and emotional influencers will be easy. The trickier part is identifying the hidden things in your daily routine that have been accepted as "safe" and "non-threatening" to your thinking, thought processes, and feelings. This is when it becomes slightly more challenging. Becoming aware of negative external influences and factors (i.e. the news playing on the radio or TV) takes practice, but becomes easier with time and patience. Making sure things are not playing in the background will eliminate a previously unknown source of physical discomfort and stress.

What we are going to create is an awareness of your feelings and sensations. The key is to be aware of changes and shifts, while tuning into what's going on around you. The reason for the news fast is to eliminate the obvious, as well as to become conscious of what you may have never paid any attention to previously. As I sit writing and thinking about this, I realize I can hear the TV in the background from one room and the sounds of what my son is listening to on his computer in another. I may be more aware than most, but I really wasn't consciously aware until I thought about it, as I am writing right now. Having the radio/TV/internet playing in the background is something not usually noticed consciously. Subconsciously however, everything is absorbed and processed. This is why it's important to become aware of changes in emotions and body feelings, and then realize that something caused it somewhere. Once you become less overwhelmed and reactive, you'll be more fascinated with how many seemingly innocent things actually cause reactions in your body. Thoughts and feelings are not as random as you may have believed. They are normally triggered by something seemingly innocent that occurs in the too often accepted environment. If you "connect the dots" you'll realize that a random thought is not random at all.

You must become aware of your environment and how it can affect the body. One way to control this is to look at obvious negative aspects in your life and limit or eliminate them. The media and all the ways it's utilized is a direct doorway to your subconscious. We pull our guard down and consider most media sources as trustworthy, causing our filter doorways to collapse and allowing our subconscious to open up. We allow whatever they want to show us, tell us, promote to us, or even fabricate to us, to become our new (in many cases) unquestioned reality. These doorways must be guarded at all times. Otherwise, your emotional state will be controlled by the next news story, the next reporter's attitude, or the fear used to shock you in a desperate attempt to get your attention.

Guarding what you "let in" is not an option, it is vital to the way you think and feel. Is it difficult to do? Not really. It does take practice and consistency that in time and with repetition will become second nature. We are looking for awareness at this point. From there we can begin to notice the changes going on within ourselves. Always look to the environment when things don't feel right. Make sure not to blame the environment or anyone else for that matter, as that never makes anything better. Become aware of how you're feeling and then you can make environmental changes that'll prevent many of the same reactions in the future.

Thoughts Come Before ANY Emotional Reactions

Before any emotional reaction, there is always a thought first. Today I met with a 21-year-old man who was full of anxiety and quite negative. Several years ago, he experienced something very significant and he couldn't stop thinking about it. When I spoke about those who watched a lot of news having difficulty controlling their thoughts, he was more than slightly surprised. He was a self-confessed "newsaholic," who started each day watching the 24-hour news channel. He was even more taken aback when I stated I didn't watch the news. It's interesting when the most obvious things are so unobvious! You cannot be positive when you surround yourself with negativity. I have yet to see a positive news station that shows great stories about great people doing great things. You can only be as positive as the things you say, things you think, and the things that you surround yourself with on a daily basis.

It is an easy process that's as simple as you using it and limiting the negativity in your surroundings. If you're not feeling as good as you want, then turn off the negativity and turn on those people and things that will create positive thoughts and feelings in your life. You may not be able to shut it off 100%, but 50% is actually 100% better than you were. Remember, we always focus on the improvements no matter how much or how slight. They are the steps in the right direction. Once you start, focus on the improvement and the changes that you are creating each day.

Elimination of All Negative Environmental Influences

To eliminate ALL negative environmental influences might be a little difficult. The problem is when people don't realize what the negative influences are and actually offer an accepting welcome to them. This might include family and relatives who are always full of drama. This could be pessimistic parents who grew up in a different generation and are cynical about everything and everyone. Some people tell me how their work places are full of "bad energy." Their bosses or associates always seem to complain about something, which brings them down. It goes on and on.

You may not be able to eliminate many of these negative influences for a variety of reasons. It might be tough to avoid parents and siblings, who sometimes just show up at your door. However, there are steps you can take to limit the obvious stressful circumstances. Start by eliminating things one day at a time. Focus on the change and then you can look forward to the future. It really is a straightforward process; although, you need to keep it simple. Don't complicate matters. Focus on one situation at a time and remember not to be too hard on yourself, as you begin to create the changes. As Buddha said, "If you take care of each moment, you will take care of all time."Always work on the improvements, giving yourself credit along the way, even when you know there's more to do and accomplish.

Taking Care of Each Moment – The Beginning of Happiness

We are trying to eliminate all these negative influences to gain control of the mental arena where all our thoughts operate. By removing the negative, we'll make room for the positive. That's what we are really trying to do. That's the mission. Remove the stuff we don't want or need to make room for the good stuff that makes us feel fulfilled. Namely, happy thoughts, positive thinking, and surrounding ourselves with some great people.

It's like watching a movie: a happy movie will make you feel happy, while a sad one will make you feel sad. When you change the movie, it changes the emotional response and then the way you feel. This will change your life forever. It really is that easy. The sooner you do it, the sooner you will believe in it and the faster it will change.

"Cynics will say there are no good people out there. And if you read the papers and watch TV news you could be convinced of that. But there are good people."
Jan Karon

Chapter Nine

News "Fasting"

Stopping the Negativity
From Entering Your Mind

News has become so negative and so quick to report with high definition images, on the scene live video and interviews that it has become a negative information overload.

This is why I always recommend my clients suffering from stress should go on a "news fast." I get clients telling me all the time that they cancelled their newspaper and began to notice a difference in their lives. One woman not only cut off her subscription, in order to eliminate future harassment from a pushy salesperson, listed her reason for termination as "moving out of the region." She recognized what I was saying in regards to all the negativity and how it was playing through her head; thus, affecting everything else she did.

I let my newspaper subscription lapse some time ago. It's interesting what happens when you do that. A few weeks later, the sales department calls to entice you with all sorts of offers and discounts. I'll admit I got pulled into that and renewed, only to let it lapse again several months down the line. One day, a salesperson called to tell me how much I was missing and how much I needed the newspaper to be "connected" to the world. I decided to play along with her a bit by stating that I wasn't missing anything. Her beloved paper was a source of negativity, sadness, doom and gloom, and was putting fear into the community's people. I repeated that I wasn't missing anything! At the time, I was sitting in my kitchen watching my two new cute puppies. At that exact moment, I realized the salesperson was right. There really was something missing: my puppies, Lucky and Layla, had nothing to pee on!

I ordered the paper and used it to train them. The paper has since lapsed and we have no intention of renewing it. Nonetheless, the next month, I was surprised that the newspaper was attempting to recruit us again by offering a one-month free subscription, without even asking. Thankfully, it too has expired; even more thankfully, Lucky and Layla are housebroken!

Your Environment – It Can Make You or Break You

There are always exceptions to every rule and there are interpretations to every concept and idea. One of my clients recently came to me about some marital issues, where she had realized her mistakes and was now working to correct them. She also told me how her husband conveniently quoted tidbits from recent books that pertained to his version of the story. Unfortunately, the parts he was quoting only caused more of a wedge between them, as it was apparent he wasn't dealing with the issue at hand or attempting to find a solution. By his actions, he was simply trying to justify his position in a desperate attempt to prove himself right!

The goal of this work and all my work is to help people make things whole. This might be for the first time, or it could mean making it whole once again. Thought Shifting will allow you to get your life together, mend relationships, and bring back families. These concepts are meant to release and remove the stresses of the past, as well as identify what really creates and locks in the emotional confusion. This is freedom in thought, starting with your mind, then into your body. Apply these concepts with an open mind and you'll soon receive some amazing results, which you may have never believed possible.

It is possible and you can make it happen.

I have found if you take some responsibility for whatever situation you're now experiencing, it changes everything and gives you the power to shift into a new beginning. There are people who have experienced particular difficulties that many of us may find difficult to imagine, let alone comprehend. I know how you're feeling because I've been through it with many clients over the years. I worked for quite some time with the local police department's Victim Services Unit, helping victims of major crimes to remove emotional issues, traumas, post-traumatic stress disorder (PTSD), and various other forms of stress. It might seem difficult, but if you can take some responsibility (this is NOT granting acceptance), even though you know the situation wasn't your fault, everything will change. It'll change how you look at life and how you're feeling. Then, you'll NEVER be a victim, no matter what.

Freeing yourself from the thoughts of being stuck and unable to do anything is in itself empowering. That's the idea of this work: to empower and enlighten you to see the light of change. I want you to be aware of it, grasp it, work it, and use it to help yourself and others.

The Teacher is Always Ready

There is an old saying that "when the student is ready, the teacher will appear."The way it should read is that "the teachers are always there; it's the students that aren't ready." Let yourself be a ready student of life and all its lessons. Let your journey be one to empower you, when you begin to understand what you've learned and the opportunities to learn more everyday with everyone and in every situation.

There may be some frustrations caused by others, who may not want your new wisdom and understanding. Hence, the saying "when the student is ready, YOU the teacher, will appear and be ready to help them." It's necessary to try and do everything to help others, but don't become disillusioned if they aren't ready or are closed minded. You will more clearly understand why this is after applying the concepts presented here, first to yourself before anyone else.

When I first started working these processes into my own life, I became very excited to see the quick and wonderful changes. I was trying to help everyone! Some listened, while others did not. It seemed the ones who needed it most were often the least responsive or interested. However, I did notice that when clients came to see me in my office, it was easy to share and explain these powerful life-changing methods. Still, a few didn't seem to want to get results. Fascinating! Why would someone not want to feel better if they were going through personal situations that were making them suffer physically and mentally?

That's when I discovered the term "secondary gain." This is when someone actually receives a benefit when there's a problem. Let me give you an example. If a boy gets attention from his mother when he gets a bellyache, you might find that whenever he needs attention his belly will actually ache. I'm not suggesting an imagined and perceived discomfort; I'm talking about an actual ache. At first, it might be an automatic response without the physical pain. After repeated instances, it can become an ingrained subconscious reaction, which shows up whenever the child needs attention.

When Issues and Problems Serve Some Legitimate Purposes

It doesn't mean everyone with an issue or ache and pain has secondary gain; although, I'm convinced many do. For that reason, when I'm removing an issue, I also look at the possible life changes that will occur once it's eliminated; subsequently, eliminating all the negative attention it once commanded. Think of those people who have pain or discomfort and how they talk about it over and over again. It's like the only attention they ever get. Even when someone comes to see me to remove something, I have to ask if it's really okay to remove this issue. Will it be okay to no longer associate with it? What will it mean when others can no longer ask you about it? What will it mean when you can no longer say "NO" because there is no longer an issue? These are some real issues with real repercussions that can create different and further problems. But what it really does is to reveal the REAL issues that need to be addressed. Even though an issue is a problem, it has often allowed a type of needed survival.

I had a client once with elderly parents, who was stressed and busy with her own life. She spent a considerable amount of time with her folks taking them to doctor appointments and various tests. She told me how they'd always call to tell her about the newest appointment they needed a ride to or their latest medical test results. My client was tired and frustrated. As we spoke, I learned she had a very close relationship with her parents, but I also realized the only time she'd see them was for medical reasons; otherwise, she would never go visit.

It became obvious the reason they called was to talk to her and the medical excuses were their way of keeping in contact. It was also when my client would listen, showing care and compassion. I said, "Your parents need you, but don't know how to get your attention without a medical reason." My client looked at me and gave me this little grin. She understood. During subsequent sessions when we mentioned her parents, she would smile and felt very good about them. Unfortunately, her mother passed away six months later. Yet, even in the face of this sad situation, my client was so relieved that we'd done the work. It allowed her to feel a closeness she hadn't previously experienced, because of what she thought were her parents' constant demands and need to be in contact. There was need by her parents that resulted in a certain behaviour; when it was understood, it changed everything for my client. She soon felt great about the time she spent with her parents and looked at that time in a totally different way.

Let me tell you another story about secondary gain, that has to do with severe, almost total incapacitating, pain. A friend asked if I could help his neighbour who was in rough shape. I said I would gladly see him and was told nothing further about this individual's physical condition. A few weeks later, this man shows up and fills out the basic intake form that asks a few questions to describe their current circumstances. I asked him into my office and he sort of wobble-walked across the floor carrying the clipboard. I watched his face and with this unusual "rigid sensitivity" tried to slowly get into the chair. I reached to get the clipboard and kept looking at him, observing the situation. I didn't even glance at what he'd written down. There was something here that didn't seem right.

I made a comment that he must be in a lot of pain and his face grimaced, as he nodded in agreement. Again, I immediately knew something wasn't right. So I asked if it was all right to ask him a question, to which he replied I could ask him anything. "And you won't get upset if I inquire about something very personal?"He repeated that it was perfectly okay.

I leaned towards him and said, "Is the lawsuit over yet?" The words were barely out of my mouth, when he glared and screamed at me, "Screw the money!" I told him that I thought he deserved the money and was most likely entitled to it for all his suffering. I then advised him that after years of this incredible pain, it would be very difficult to get any relief, as his settlement depended on how much he was suffering and subsequent future lost earnings. If this man removed any pain, it would hurt him financially because of how the system is set up. Again, this is what I call secondary gain. It's not as if he wasn't in pain; trust me, he was. But it's difficult to create a change when the old ways and habits are actually fulfilling a needed purpose. I told this man it would be best to make another appointment after the lawsuit was settled, when he would be better prepared to eliminate the pain from which he was suffering. This man also may have wanted to add me to his list of what didn't work – I guess he really didn't know who he came to see! I always like to look at the bigger picture and find what the real motivating factor in one's subconscious is.

This does NOT mean that everyone in chronic or prolonged pain is experiencing it from secondary gain. This was simply an example that I had come into the office. How did I know there was a lawsuit? It was just something I sensed, because NO ONE walked the way this poor man did!

This is an extreme example of secondary gain; yet, I think you can get an idea of how it actually works. It is also a very common reason some people hang on to their old thinking and old ways.

Root Cause vs. Symptoms

When this happens, you must look deeper than the presenting symptoms. As a rule, the problem presented is not the real problem. I often say that the real issues are usually several weeks away after the first visit. The initial things people focus on will be the issue at hand. For instance, it might be their pain, their headaches, their insomnia, their anxiety, etc. These are the results of the actual issues and the actual problem. These symptoms have become so dominant in one's thoughts that they become the real issue. It makes sense if you think about it, because before the symptom you were fine, so take away the symptom and everything should be back on track again.

For example: If you have a garden hose that can only hold so much pressure and then you increase it to over its limit, you can expect problems. Perhaps a leak here or there or a bulge in the hose would be a normal outcome. So what's the solution? Of course we want to fix the leak; but if we do that and walk away, what would you then expect to happen next? Another bulge or leak somewhere else is the most likely result. Therefore, the only real solution is to reduce the pressure in the hose to prevent more leaks. Stopping the leak will temporarily fix your current problem, but cannot stop further issues in the future.

The same goes with your problems when you do something similar. If you only go after the health issue (the pain, the insomnia, the anxiety), you're doing nothing except masking the issue, while the root cause remains. Medicating and masking symptoms will stop the immediate issue; however, in most cases, it will not prevent something else from developing. Yes, you must stop the bleeding, but you also must stop more from happening in the weeks, months, and years ahead.

Most medical doctors will tell you that stress disorders are one of the leading causes of medical visits. I look at it this way: stress causes tension, tension causes illness, illness causes disease, and disease causes death. Stress is not something to be overlooked or accepted. It is very common for my clients to claim they're stressed, only to add, "But nothing out of the ordinary." What is THAT supposed to mean? I take it to mean unnecessary stress is now an acceptable and expected part of these clients' lives.

There can be nothing farther from the truth.

Our goal is to recognize and identify negative thoughts that create the feelings behind stress in the body, and to use specific techniques to neutralize and eliminate it at the root cause. This is our game plan. It'll be easy to implement and apply to your day-to-day thought processes.

One key factor is to catch thoughts before they go off into an opposite direction from where you really desire to be. It's like going down a slide and you can't stop. The further down the slide you get, the faster you seem to be going in the wrong direction. It's always easier to stop the ride at the beginning of the slide / negative thought.

One of the major obstacles people encounter is the beginning of the starting to let go of negative thinking and thought processes. For many, the first step of anything is considered the hardest. This might occur because the problem no longer feels like an issue or a major deal, due to complacency or acceptance. The process of releasing these things and truly letting them go will become much easier once it begins. In the meantime, many individuals continually let thoughts go negative and continue in the wrong direction, without ever realizing they can do anything about it. The more you let a negative thought flow in the wrong direction, the more momentum it builds, and then the more difficult it becomes to change it. Negative thoughts can start so innocently and in a minor way. However, if they remain unchecked, you run the risk of compounding the negativity and all the issues that'll follow the negative thought patterns. Negativity breeds negativity. Remember, it is easier to catch these thoughts early on and it's never too late to change them, no matter how far along they've come.

A big barrier in creating these simple changes is a lack of understanding how thoughts can steamroll into something far greater than people know how to handle. Thoughts can't be taken lightly and why should they? They create your reality and no one should be in charge of your reality except YOU. Thoughts are more powerful than physical items because thoughts create things. Try this: No matter where you are at this moment, look around and begin to realize everything in your environment was actually first created in someone's mind. That's right, everything. Before there's any action to create, there has to be the action of thinking and imagining. Thinking sets the wheels in motion. It creates answers and solutions when there are none. It stretches the mind and causes people to become creative. **In fact, thought is the source of all creation.**

I also want you to become aware of anything that causes confusion in your mind. This usually shows up as a problem, an issue, a dilemma, even a serious situation. All of these can cause confusion. To me, confusion is probably the best thing that can ever happen to you. Why? Because it wakes us out of the trance state we often slip into. Think about it. Confusion makes you stop, look around, assess what's going on, and make changes. That's why I love confusion, as it's the only thing that can make you stop and pay attention, literally waking you up. When everything is going great, people don't usually look to improve their lives. They don't ask questions when things are all in order; nonetheless, when they're confused, look out! There is a calmness, a blank stare, an eerie silence at the beginning before an awakening. It's the immediate desire to change something that just broke, suddenly ended, or suddenly appeared. It's anything out of your normal routine that confuses you and wakes you up. If you're confused or have been lately, I am so happy for you! This is the time to harness your power and change your life, to take back your power. Once again, it all starts with a single thought: the desire and necessity to change. The shock of a reality you no longer like. This is confusion. This is the beginning of all change and the awakening to a new reality.

Take Back Your Power

That's the power of thoughts and the power of your thinking. It's also the power you need to create what you imagine and desire. This must not be taken lightly, nor should it be. To create the desired changes in your life, you must first work with the very basis of the creation of your reality. It's all based on the way you think, which will determine how you feel and this will change everything forever.

I often call thoughts "the final frontier." People are handcuffed by negativity and their beliefs in what they can't have and achieve. If you realize that what you think about you'll attract, it puts a whole new significance to those random thoughts flying in and out of your head all day long. What you think about and focus on is what your amazingly powerful mind will attract and do everything it can to achieve. It must be remembered that the mind can't process a negative, so if you think about negative things and they happen, you really are successful. When you focus on positive things, they too will happen and you will be successful. Either way, you'll get what you're focusing on, no matter whether it's good or not.

By learning how thoughts work and the power they hold in the creation of one's reality, it should become a mission in a person's self-actualization and desire for true happiness. One does not need to strive towards this pinnacle of "total" happiness and joy to benefit from these processes, but it's a necessary step to focus on the positive to begin any journey.

Many people reading this only want to be happy. I feel for you. I believe this is the first step in the right direction. One step forward begins and completes all journeys. Let these steps be your map of many possibilities, so you can navigate through the myriad of routes and destinations. Some may desire to journey far and wide, while others may only want to keep to themselves in their own private world with an inner circle of family and friends. Whatever your desire, it's possible when it exists in your mind. You cannot create anything greater than your thoughts. You cannot climb higher than your beliefs. Together you can have unlimited possibilities when they are both on the same team and on the same page.

This is all about doing the little things that will give you the big results. These methods will remove those random negative thoughts and allow you to replace them with positive ones of what you truly desire.

I never like to tell a person what to think. I feel that a person's own ideas and revelations are always the deepest and most meaningful. The problem we have now is that thoughts are no longer pure. They have become confused and no longer are a reflection of one's true desires. The head and the heart have split. The desires of a person's true meaning and spirit are no longer the guiding light of one's true passions, hopes, and dreams. Instead, they've become tainted and spoiled by the thoughts of others and their negativity. People outthink their inner heart's desire, talked out of their dreams by thoughts that originate or belong to someone else. What others believe we should be becomes a doctrine that dictates thoughts and behaviours, which ultimately shackles our soul.

Negativity is the poison of all thoughts, dreams, and desires. It spoils the fruits of passion and possibilities. It weakens spirits and souls to levels of worry and disbelief. It takes wind from the sails of young and old, leaving them floating aimlessly in an ocean of regret, fear, and frustration.

Learning to control thoughts is like having a personal lifeboat to cling on to amidst all the confusion after a mental storm washes you ashore. When situations seem like they couldn't get any worse, controlling your thoughts will set you free.

Freedom from all confusion, worry, and possibility is one thought away. One thought to begin a road of change and transformation. From there you can build and create your future, your possibilities, and live the dreams you once were afraid to imagine.

This is why thoughts are the final frontier and an area people know the least about. The mind is the least known by modern medicine and I'm not sure it will ever be truly understood. It's like trying to find God. The harder you look, the less you see; but when you have faith and belief, it's all around you, everywhere and in everything, including yourself.

"*Through pride we are ever deceiving ourselves. But deep down below the surface of the average conscience a still, small voice says to us, something is out of tune.*"
Carl Jung

Chapter Ten

The Inner Voice

How It Works and Why It Has A Mind of Its Own!

To control the inner voice is to control your life. Think about it. The inner voice is the key to happiness. I remember a time when I was not happy. I didn't feel safe and wasn't in control. In fact, I was confused, scared, and wasn't in charge of my inner voice. Plus, I had a "busy mind." Now, having a busy mind isn't a problem. It's having a negative busy mind that's the problem. You can never have too many positive thoughts; yet, one negative thought can keep you up for days.

Let me recount my situation for you.

I had just graduated from a great university, but felt as if I'd been thrown out of a moving bus more than supposedly a prepared, educated young man. I had a background formulated in business and psychology; yet, I didn't feel equipped for the world. I had good professors, great friends, and incredible parents; so why did I feel this way?

If I think about it, I had a doubting and negative inner voice. In retrospect, although the education was very good, the teachings obviously were not. "How so?" you may ask. Most of our educational background consists of attending high school, maybe college or university, some graduate school. I had all of that as well. In these types of environments, we're taught certain subjects by people who had plenty of experience or none at all.

Some teachers taught, while others simply presented. If you consider all the teachers you had, all the courses you took, and all the books you studied, one thing I can tell you with certainty is that no one ever taught you how to think! It's an assumed "given" that people know how to think and make sense out of whatever is being communicated. Your thinking is made up of your thoughts. Your thoughts are your life. A person who is thinking negatively will feel as if their life is unfulfilling, unsatisfying, and in extreme cases, not worthy of living. It begins a spiral of negativity linked to the previous negative thought. This is why negativity breeds negativity like a virus. I once heard someone describe negative thoughts as, "a computer virus downloaded during a session of life." I agree, as for most of us, it isn't the hardware (the body) that's the problem; it's the software (the mind).

You can never be better than your thoughts. Everything is what you think.

This is the missing link. It's your thoughts and your thinking. To understand how thinking works and to know how to change thoughts is the key to success. In order to feel great, happy, and fulfilled you must learn to control your thinking. It seems that no matter where you are in life, everyone assumes you know how to think. This could not be farther from the truth. I know because I've worked with some very powerful and influential people in government, society, and professional athletes. Even with all their successes, there is always one little issue: they didn't know how to control their thinking. When this happens, it makes it easier for the thoughts of others surrounding you to become your thoughts. Unfortunately, it's usually the opposite of positive. What you see, hear, or experience will become your thought processes and your thinking patterns.

People are not born negative. Thoughts and thinking are learned. You will learn from your environment. Negativity breeds negativity. This is why we talked earlier about how managing your environment is the first step to controlling your thinking and your emotional state. This is how thinking starts. It is the direct result of being exposed to other people and events. It creates your reality. It creates your belief system and points of reference. Every word you speak and hear references back to what your interpretation of that word means to you. This is why you'll get different responses from different people who have experienced the same incident at the same time. It's all based on your interpretation, dependant on your own point of reference and past experiences.

The key is not continuing in the direction others have taken us. I'm not saying you can't listen to others. We can learn from others, but learning negativity is not a lesson; it's a behaviour and a habit that may feel more like a curse. The solution? Awareness and then changing the negative inner voice.

Changing the Negative Inner Voice

We have looked at two parts of Thought Shifting so far. The first dealt with the things that you say whenever you open your mouth and everything you talk about. The important thing is controlling and understanding everything you say; especially, things that used to be thought of as "innocent" automatic responses. The second part was becoming aware of your environment and how everything and everyone has an effect on you.

This next part is all about controlling the inner voice, how to change it, and redirect any negativity. It is a powerful process we need to keep as simple as possible. You should have already been implementing the above two techniques to create changes in your thinking. This third process of converting the inner voice will allow everything else to make sense and put the pieces together.

By only implementing the first two techniques and lifestyle improvements, there would often be times of lingering thoughts and trails of negativity, which need to be redirected.

The key to your success and happiness will be to control the very voice that lives in your head. It knows your deepest darkest secrets, fears, and concerns. It can make or break you in any situation that you might find yourself in. Depending on the direction it goes, there is anything from hope and confidence to fear and despair. I don't have to convince anyone of the advantages of having the inner voice of a positive, happy, and hopeful person. Positive people have busy minds too, but they are busy in a different way. There's not a positive person I've ever met who wanted to change their thought processes. Thoughts attract and you get what you think of, good or bad. It doesn't matter to the subconscious, because its role is not to determine the quality or to filter your thoughts. Good or bad, you are sending energy out towards whatever you're focusing on. This is the issue. Negative thinking doesn't mean that everything negative will show up, just as thinking of winning the lottery means you'll actually win it. I do suggest that if you think you'll never win, don't buy any tickets because you'll just beat yourself up if you lose. Many people, who don't think they will win, don't play; therefore, they're definitely not going to win. Someone has to win every contest and every competition, so why not you or me? Have some fun; don't bet the farm, but play with some hope! Someone has to win every contest and every competition, so why not you or me?

Every Thought Is A Choice – Your Choice

Remember, if you don't want 100% of your thoughts to come true, then you have to understand Thought Shifting and apply the processes. Whatever you think about or focus on, you're sending energy and attracting it back towards you. For many that is a scary thought! The first two processes we worked on will place you in a very good position, but it doesn't control the inner voice. Hence, we developed a process to reprogram and redirect the inner voice quickly and instantly towards what it is you actually desire. You will particularly need and want this next step.

This third process is to convert the inner voice when it starts to go negative. Many people think thoughts are random. It might be possible but it is most likely improbable. There are many more reasons why a person's thoughts go negative. It might be from a locked in memory triggered by something or someone. It might be from a story you saw, read, or were told. Maybe it's a negative friend, relative, co-worker, or neighbour. Perhaps it's the radio that is on in the background. It can even be the vehicle in front of you at a stop light. Anything and everything can trigger a new direction, a different thought, a smile, a laugh, a worry, or a concern. Whatever it is and no matter what the cause, when your mind goes negative it must be stopped and redirected. The sooner, the better. Having a negative thought is one thing, letting it linger in your mind is something much more serious. It's all about knowing you can do something with that thought and then knowing what to do.

We have covered the areas that cause negativity and how to control and change the environmental factors, which often happens subtlety and without realizing it. We now know how it affects and creates our thought processes. People are carried away in a moment or relationship or argument, losing sight of the bigger picture of what negativity is really doing to them. At the time, they just want to get through the situation and move on. We even get entangled in others' "stuff" and fight their battles; however, trying to win every battle presented will always make you lose the war. Being caught up in negativity is like falling into a whirlpool, being drawn into a spiralling whirlwind that seems impossible to get out of. That is unless you know how to get out, by understanding what to do and when to do it.

Thought Shifting IS the Answer

Once you understand what's going on around you, it's time to cut your losses and get out of the situation. Your well-being, health, and quality of life, as well as its length, depends on it. There will be many situations where, even when controlling your environment, saying only what you want, and talking as positive as possible, your mind will still have its moments of doubt. Happiness is a choice and a decision, just as are thinking positive thoughts. Once you've created the necessary environmental changes in your personal life, it should be noted that everyone else around you will not have changed as much as you. I say "not as much" because I'm implying that they have changed or that your change will influence them.

How is it possible that they've changed? A person's perception of anything or anyone creates the thoughts we have about it or them. Some individuals will be changed, because interacting with your new attitude and your controlled comments will also allow them to become more positive. There will be others you've innocently accepted as "just the way they are" or perhaps it is in the form of a relationship; such as, family, which makes it difficult to remove these individuals from your life. This latter group may make you angry and frustrated by their consistent negativity, but be careful not to allow them to suck you in. There is a saying that goes, "The more you know, the more you will realize you do not know." If everyone has a cold and you cure yourself, it doesn't mean the others are healed. Becoming positive is like becoming healed. Remember, most negative people do not think they're negative. Some are clueless, while many tell me they are happy 75% of the time. The problem is that 25% of the time they are 100% negative. This is not acceptable for happiness.

Happiness starts with you. This means doing things right for yourself first and then helping others. A negative person, such as a relative, may be difficult to remove from your life. We all have them. We all know them. They will frustrate you even more once you know this information. Accept them for who they are, while knowing they have zero desire to change. Ignorance is not bliss; although, for them, they've survived this long thinking and doing what they do on a daily basis. There is acceptance on their own personal level. It's interesting how total strangers often have more success creating change in those who don't want our help. The amount you care about someone has little to do with your success. It really depends on the relationship and whether it's a "looking up" or a "looking down" situation. It will be easier with individuals who look up to us (i.e. kids to parents).

Those who look down towards us will be more difficult (i.e. parents to their children). There are always exceptions and you shouldn't assume anything; including, assuming that this is what you will get. My advice is to presume you can help everyone but don't believe that you need to. It will make you suffer more than if you never tried to help anyone.

"You cannot quickly change the world, BUT you can quickly change YOUR world by changing your thoughts."
~ Rick Saruna

As you can see, hear, sense, and feel, there are many situations where you can apply this new information and help others. You want to share it with them and the world. Keep in mind, every great discovery is met with some resistance and ridicule. Creating change in other people's behaviours and thought processes may not always be as easy as it was for you. These techniques and methods are life changing for those who want to accept them. You'll be surprised at how simple they are and how they work immediately. Truly amazing. More amazing (and more frustrating) will be those you care about who aren't interested in accepting and implementing these powerful processes. YOU have to be accepting of their wishes, yet not accepting of their negativity. There is no harm in trying to help someone be more positive or show them "the way." Just know when to cut your losses.

I use the example of an individual attempting to save a drowning victim. If you're not careful, they will try to unintentionally drown you, as their panicky survival mode kicks in. I truly believe people do the best they can in life based on what they know. I look at it this way: Do people really want to be sick and miserable? Before you jump to any conclusions or think of a specific person you know, honestly consider this: if they didn't think the way they do, would they be the same way they are? Of course not.

This is why it's so important to change the negative inner voice, that one part of you that decides how to process a comment, situation, or event that is current, perceived coming, or even past. Like a game of bumper pool, the events of our life have a cause and effect. Thought after thought depending on how the last one was processed, determining where you'll go next with them. All thoughts seem to be left to chance, with or without reason. Is this the way to live? Is this the direction to go through life, trying to make a difference for loved ones and yourself? How can happiness be achieved when you are affected by the thoughts and actions of others? Are you waking up in the morning waiting to see what others are thinking, in order to determine how you're feeling for the rest of the day? Now, THAT is the definition of madness! Not only is that the wrong way to start each day, it also empowers the other person's emotions no matter if they are good, bad, or downright messed up! Let's avoid this ritual at all costs, okay?

Through Thought Shifting, you can take control of your thoughts and your life. It is very important to not allow your environment (and the people within it) to determine how you think and feel. Someone has to be in control and that someone has to be you. When it comes to how you think and feel, the Captain of the ship is you. You have always been in control; it's just that no one told you before. Well, I'm telling you now. No one empowered you with this information early in life. Imagine telling children they had power, the ability to decide what they wanted, when they wanted it, and how much they wanted. Then told they had the ability and right to say "Yes" and the ability and right to say, "No."

WOW! Think of the potential. Think of the chaos!

"Your time is limited, so don't waste it living someone else's life. Don't be trapped by dogma - which is living with the results of other people's thinking. Don't let the noise of others' opinions drown out your own inner voice. And most important, have the courage to follow your heart and intuition."
Steve Jobs

Chapter Eleven

Breaking FREE From The Control of Others

It is all about control. You've been controlled for years and by many people. The truth is no one empowered you. No one told you that you're amazing and incredible. No one advised you there are no mistakes, only feedback. No one told you how powerful you are, how you can get what you want, and that dreams do come true. No one told you because it was of no benefit to them to do so. If they had, they'd lose their ability to shape your thoughts and have even less control of your environment. Giving you something they themselves fear and have no knowledge of, does not work for a person supposedly in control. As these individuals can't control their own thinking, they'll always try to manage their environment. This is why whenever I have control freaks in the office seeking change, I know the first thing they need to do is change their thoughts and their thinking. Unfortunately, WE were their environment they needed to control in order to think they had control of their thoughts. Clinically, I have yet to meet a "control freak" (I say this not in a negative way

143

because many clients call themselves that) who was in control of their thought processes. To control your thoughts is to control your life. To attempt to control only your environment in the hopes of having control is a time bomb waiting to detonate. Eventually things will totally explode out of your control, disrupting the perception of the balance you never had. Once a person controls their thoughts, their life changes, peacefulness emerges, and the external environment becomes less important. You will sleep better, and then headaches, aches, and pain are reduced and often eliminated. Your life will then begin and you'll soon forget the unrest of the past. It will be an amazing time in your life.

You must make a conscious effort to realize that everything that comes at you has the potential to change your thoughts and thinking. The media intentionally does this via press releases, corporate advertising, and various groups spreading their agenda (not your agenda - their agenda). Things like this affect people who don't control their thought processes (this includes anyone who is not aware). Problems arise when you interact with the countless number of people in your environment who say or do things that affect your thoughts, your thinking, and the way you feel.

The key here is to be FREE. In order to do so, you must learn to control your thought processes and become aware of your environment, as well as your inner voice. This next process I want to go over is a technique that will work on changing your inner voice through a self-retraining process. Retraining because the initial training you received was not yours. It was the programming we were all subjected to by people with their own desires or having followed the desires others put into them. It can really get pretty deep if we let it.

All Issues Are Old Issues

In reality, all issues are old issues. Everything that's ever happened to you has happened before this moment in time. It is in the past. The past is over and done. The problem is most individuals don't like the way things ended. If everything had ended the way you wanted it, you would never go back there. So basically, they are unresolved issues that can't be resolved by thinking about them. Memory is actually a regression. In a true regression, a person's mind goes back and becomes the age when it was experienced, with all those same limited resources. Therefore, every time you think about a past issue, you immediately revert to that period, allowing all those lost feelings of helplessness and hopelessness to return with a vengeance. It's like déjà vu all over again!

What is the answer? What can you do? How can you stop the madness and the pain? It really isn't that difficult. If we understand the concepts and follow a few simple instructions, everything can and will change.

When it comes to removing stress, there are times where a stubborn or stuck emotional issue(s) causes recurring negative thoughts or memories. We are hardwired by emotions to lock in negative experiences, in order to avoid them in the future. This is what has allowed us to survive as a species. Memories that are emotionalized get locked into the subconscious; thereby, making them timeless. This is best demonstrated in how a phobia works. It usually begins with a situation that's experienced with an intense emotion. Emotions come from the subconscious, where there is no time or space. So an emotionalized memory is a subconscious reminder that gets locked into timelessness. This is to prompt you subconsciously to avoid something that's unpleasant, uncomfortable, or outright life threatening.

Many of these locked in emotions are fears and worries that become a person's belief system. They can be overwhelming and all consuming. Thought Shifting works in any situation; however, various emotional issues and their corresponding beliefs can wreak havoc on a person's attempt to become positive. Negative issues and beliefs will often draw a person back into the past. It is a known fact that when you change a person's belief system, you change them at a deep subconscious level. Therefore, it's important to remain as constant and consistent as possible with Thought Shifting. When there are deep issues involving trauma, phobias, and the like, there are methods that can be utilized to remove them.

In my clinic, I do several things to help people quickly remove emotional issues and change their belief system. I call it Rapid Emotional Release (RER). I am now teaching this system to others who want to learn this amazing process, which can change a person's belief system no matter what the issue(s) or from how long ago. The system works swiftly to get rid of even the deepest emotional issues. I developed this process that essentially defies all conventional therapies and processes of emotional change and freedom. I use it alongside Thought Shifting because in the end it isn't just about removing the emotion; it's about changing the thoughts that make up one's existence. A person's existence is in their head. A person who controls their thinking will control their life. Ideally, I like to remove the emotional attachment to a negative thought so the thought is actually forgotten, as thoughts are only made memorable through the emotions attached to them. This draws it into the timelessness of the subconscious, where emotion lives on that image, making it vividly memorized. Every time that image is remembered through various triggers, it's the attached emotion that brings you the pain, like a vivid flashback frozen in time when you couldn't or didn't control your thoughts. These emotions make you focus on something longer than needed or desired. Fears, phobia, trauma, PTSD, and all emotional issues can all be released with the Rapid Emotional Release process. This also includes things like negative beliefs that have been ingrained into someone's mind and limits their success.

Even when I do emotional work and remove the most intense traumatic memories, I still need to change a person's thoughts so they can focus on what they want, instead of what they do not want. I like to not only remove the negative emotion, but also replace it with a positive thought. We can equate this to watching a bad television program that we dislike because of something negative shown on it. If we just turn the TV off, the memory will still be lingering; but if we immediately refocus by turning the channel to something pleasant, the last channel is easy to forget. It's very difficult to still the mind. It is actually easier to busy the mind with positive thoughts than to stop the thoughts in one's mind. Positive people aren't looking to still their mind; it's only those negative people who listen to their inner voice that knows their deepest, darkest fears and secrets. These negative thoughts need to be "unemotionalized" in order to remove the memory. Emotions lock in the memory, so with "emotional release" the intensity and vividness of the memory release and fade; in most cases, it's rather quickly when done properly. Properly means the right technique with consistency and persistence. I use RER (Rapid Emotional Release), which I developed and have trained others in its methods. I also use a Tapping Technique that works on meridian points and is available on our website as a home study process. People that have done any "tapping" for emotional issues will appreciate the different style and approach that I use. It's a great technique that will walk you through some powerful changes. However, that is only a part of the overall change you desire.

Releasing Negativity Is Like Putting Out a Fire – Eventually You Must Catch the Arsonist

After you let go of an emotional issue, then what? Hope that something else doesn't pop up? This is the real issue. Putting out emotional fires is one thing, but eventually you have to catch the arsonist starting one burning negative thought after another. Ultimately, YOU MUST change thought processes to change your life, stop other people from negatively affecting you, and preventing other issues from popping up.

So the need is to stop emotionally time travelling back to the past and start to refocus and shift into the future. This is the easiest way to "change your channel" of thinking, just as turning to a more calming TV program benefits you immediately, instead of simply turning it off and trying to forget it . I like to refocus thoughts into the future. To do this one needs to understand that unlike the past, which is based on memory, the future is not. The future is based on one thing and one thing only: your imagination. Think about it: you don't remember what happened tomorrow, do you? Or next week? Or next month? Or next year? Of course not. You can't remember the future, but you can imagine it. You can imagine tomorrow, next week, next month, even next year!

Here is a question: If you knew in one year from now (not if you thought, but actually knew) that everything was going to fit perfectly together and you'd have love to give and receive, health, happiness, and peacefulness, how would you feel? I mean, you would feel GREAT! Instead, if you thought, "Oh no, what if this or what if that?"and worried about all those things living in your imagination, you'd continue to feel stressed out.

The REAL Secret to Life

Here now is the key to the secret to life. Are you ready? Forget anything else you read or heard. This is what it comes down to: If how you imagine the future determines how you feel, why do people always imagine what they don't want? The issue is that people keep going into the past, remembering those negative things they haven't been able to change, and project them into the future. It's not a surprise when they are left wondering why today is a lot like yesterday.

The process of Thought Shifting will get you out of that. Only through Thought Shifting will you be able to release the past, by refocusing your thoughts through the incredible power of your imagination. All of this will take you into the future of what you desire and deserve.

People who are stressed have a great imagination. Know why I know? It's because they keep imagining all the things they don't want to happen! I know because I used to think the same way. What happens when your mind is filled with negativity or when you listen to all the people in your life and pay too much attention to the media? You become one stressed, scared, and negative person. Your mind then projects all this negativity into the future, with its vivid imagination of things not working out and past pessimistic feelings repeating themselves. To me, THAT is way too much work!

It's time to change all that. It's time to make the decision to regain the control of our thoughts, our thinking, and to discover a freedom and peacefulness we never knew existed. That peacefulness and freedom does exist and it's very real.

It's filled with promises and amazing opportunities. It doesn't matter about your age, your situation, or the things you've been through; everything can and will change if you have the desire to let it happen, and then learn and implement these rules of the mind.

"Following our inner guidance may feel risky and frightening at first, because we are no longer playing it safe, doing what we 'should' do, pleasing others, following rules, or deferring to outside authority."
Shakti Gawain

Chapter Twelve

The Process of Reprogramming The Inner Voice

You have never been taught how or what to think. Of all the things that society has tried to teach us from Day 1, you'd think somewhere along the road there would have been a class, a lesson, a time or a place where we'd be taught how to use the most powerful part of us: our mind. I'm not sure about you, but I don't recall in any grade, class, or training that special day when I was shown how to think and get everything in life I ever wanted. This is what needs to be taught to our children and to us. Empowerment is something that would skyrocket confidence, goal achievement, happiness, and health.

It seems the mind works from a position of default. There is no system. There is no method and there's been no technique taught to us on how to change thought processes. A method to enable us to think happy, positive thoughts, and live our lives accordingly seems to have eluded our paths. Is it that no one knows how to do this because no one showed them? Or has life become so much about creating and achieving, that YOU were never taught how to "live" life?

So when your mind started to think negatively or went off on an unwanted direction, there was nothing one could do. One thought would lead to another and another, until you were so far off you forgot where you started. Sounds like an internet search where you just keep clicking away! That's about to change very shortly. I am going to help reprogram your subconscious mind in this section of Thought Shifting. This is the day in class we all seemed to have "missed." I suppose there might be a reason not to tell us how powerful we are at a young age; in case we decided to say, "No way!" too early to the establishment and to all those people who had power over us.

Now that would have changed things! So let the empowerment begin here.

How? Well, many years ago, a mentor of mine who'd spent his life studying the mind said to me, "The trained mind is a faithful servant. " This is not something many have experienced, because for a majority of people the mind is like a wild untrained animal that is very volatile. Having the mind work in a predictable way will be calming and comforting, which is something we aren't used to. There will be so many life improvements.

It's unfortunate that individuals have been disempowered by others, not always intentionally but because those who've surrounded us can often only teach what they know. That knowledge is often very limited. This starts very early. We can't expect anyone to teach us what they do not know.

Today, it is time to change all that at a deep level.

The subconscious mind is not at all complicated, which might seem a bit difficult to understand or comprehend. However, there is often simplicity in complexity and this process is easy to follow, with immediate and profound results.

Reprogramming the Subconscious

We will start our subconscious reprogramming by choosing a keyword to command the subconscious, which will therefore cause the response we desire in our mind. Instead of repeating the whole instruction over and over again, the subconscious simply needs a reminder to keep it aware of what you desire it to do. It's really quite remarkable how the subconscious is like a child who needs a request repeated to them several times. In the same manner, a child might not listen right away, and sometimes you raise your voice and increase its intensity! We don't need to get mad or upset at ourselves; we only need to use the part of repetition to keep the subconscious focused. A child can get easily diverted and distracted, losing their ability to focus on the requested task. Similarly, the subconscious mind can get distracted and lost in other thoughts drawing its attention. The concept here is "spaced repetition" to train the mind to listen or refocus on when the command is given. Just because you tell your mind to shift into another thought and it doesn't right away, doesn't mean that the process isn't working. When a child doesn't listen, do you give up or stop? No, you get their attention quickly and repeat the instruction. This is VITAL. Like you would with a child, you repeat your request until the behaviour is corrected. If you don't reinforce what you want, you lose control. You must repeat the keyword subconscious command repetitively, especially during the initial Thought Shifting training. It is important to be consistent because people need to remember to use their keyword when there is an issue confronting them. Initially, you should practice redirecting simple things and thoughts that are not overwhelming.

Remember, the key is repetition. You are training the mind to pay attention to YOU. You're the one in control and your subconscious mind will begin to respect that once you use this process with consistency and mastery. It is a simple process, so please don't complicate it!

This is also where all the pieces of this book's training will come together. It's not just a desire to stop a negative thought. There is much, much more we desire here! For many, this is the only desire. Get rid of that thought! We can and will do much better than ONLY that. This is an incredible opportunity for us to not only remove negative thoughts, but to now replace them with what we really want. If you don't like what you're watching on TV, you may just shut it off; however, you'll still have the negative images fresh in your mind. Instead, if you press the channel to something that is positive and enjoyable, it is much easier to feel better and think healthier thoughts immediately. When removing any negative thought, feeling, or sensation, you need to repeat your keyword silently or out loud, depending on where you are and who you are with at the time.

Removing Negativity is Only Part of the Solution

Removing the negativity is only part of our desire here. The real goal is to begin thinking positively and to no longer create other negative thought processes that will need to be removed later. Many people are so negative that they're in survival mode and empowerment is beyond the main goal of just getting through their day. You can do much better than that. This whole process of Thought Shifting will not only remove your negative inner voice, it'll allow you to see and create a future of possibility that will become your reality.

This process is not about "getting by" or "making it through the day." It's about removing negative thoughts and feelings and replacing them with amazing, empowering ideas and sensations. These in turn will attract the things you always wanted and can now begin to desire into your life.

This is an exciting time in your life and I am excited for you.

Removing negative thinking is imperative to both your health and happiness. However, remember that the theory is often easier than implementation. Let me explain why. You have likely been raised in negativity, experiencing traumatic events or moments you'd rather forget but cannot. Maybe you disagree with this assessment and have decided you are simply a worrier. Well in my clinic, I have heard this many times from clients proclaiming, "I'm not negative. I'm just a worrier!" My response is always, "Worried about what, things working out perfectly? Are you worried everyone is going to be okay and things will work out?" Of course not. You wouldn't worry about anything positive. All worry is negative in nature. Even though we're going to remove this negativity, you must remember that it's still successfully brought you to this point in your life. In a strange way, it's worked to keep you going. You've been relying on it, even though you don't like it. It's a habit and you've trained everyone in your life to respond to you that way too. So our retraining won't only be within ourselves, but with others all around us as well.

As I was saying, our goal will be to keep the mind busy. There's nothing wrong with a "busy mind" as long as those thoughts are the ones you want, which are positive and constructive. A negative mind is a busy mind, because it keeps looking for the worst possibilities and the next potential problem. It can be quite difficult to still a negative busy mind. So, we are NOT going to still it and we are not even going to try to. In fact, we're going to keep it busy and active. That's right, busy and active; except now, with positive thoughts and the things you want. Too many people become frustrated by trying to still their mind and blank out thoughts. That isn't our goal or our technique. Do you think happy, positive people filled with empowering thoughts are trying to still their minds? We will be replacing racing and recurring negative thoughts with new ones based on how you would prefer things to turn out. We are going to learn to convert any thought into something positive and constructive. It won't matter what the thought or situation is because you'll learn how to project it into the future, as you would expect it to be if anything was possible. Remember how we talked about the future being based on your imagination and not your memory? We have already established you have an excellent imagination, because you've been imagining all the things you don't want to happen!

We will use our keyword to direct the subconscious mind and then take the issue or situation and project it into the future, now accompanied by the thoughts or the end result we desire to have happen. The goal here is NOT to think about how you'll get there! The same way a negative thinker focuses on doom and gloom, we will focus the new thoughts of health and happiness and other similar positive end results.

Here is the subconscious instruction and direction:

You can use any word you like and even add more words later to be your keyword trigger. You can have more than one keyword, but we'll start with one to keep it simple. Keywords can be anything from, "Stop-Stop," "Delete-Delete," "Cancel-Cancel," etc. I have several words I utilize and it seems the more you do this technique, the less you need to use it later. I go back to the first keyword I ever used and taught my children, "Cancel-Cancel;" however, if that word is not something you like or if any word reminds of something negative, you can use something else, such as "Delete Delete."

Please choose your keyword right now. Got it? When you do, you can continue.

The following instructions DO NOT need to be memorized. You simply read through them and then your subconscious is ready to use them in the future.

Programming Your Subconscious Mind

Ok, here we go…

"Anytime I see something, hear something, sense or feel something I do not want to accept, keep, empower, or absorb in any way, shape, or form, I will simply say to myself my keywords *Cancel-Cancel*. Whenever I say my keywords Cancel-Cancel it will tell my subconscious mind not to accept, absorb, keep, or empower in any way, shape, or form any of these words, thoughts, images, feelings, or sensations. Instead, to release, to relax, and let go totally and completely from all levels of the my body and mind, no matter where I am, no matter what I am doing, or whoever I am with, if anyone at all." *Cancel-Cancel, Cancel-Cancel.*

That is it.

That trigger keyword is now a direct instruction to the subconscious mind. The instructions are recorded in your mind and don't need to be remembered consciously. The key is to use it with consistency and constantly. You will initially cancel just about everything and anything, then Thought

Shift a related but now totally positive thought of what you want in the future. The principle being that the future is based on your imagination and not your memory. You DO NOT remember the future, you can only imagine it. So if it's based only on your imagination, we're now going to imagine what we want, even if we don't know how it will happen. This is very, very important.

Awareness – Then Action – Gets Results

The process works by becoming aware of thoughts and knowing you have a system to control and change thinking to create the life and future you desire. Our focus is not trying to change the past but to enjoy the now by empowering the future. The whole concept of living in the now is great, but if you thought the future was not going to work out, it will be impossible to relax enough to enjoy the now. The way we think about the future and its possibilities creates our NOW.

It is important to realize the future is based on our thought processes and our thinking. Negative thoughts will make you perceive the future in a negative way and that'll make you feel negative right now. Our outlook on the future will determine how we feel in this moment right now. Our outlook is our attitude and our thoughts. Control these and everything changes. Changing thoughts is the process of practicing the technique with repetition in all situations.

There is a moment of truth to cancelling out and shifting negative thoughts. Remember, you are retraining the negative inner mind that historically has been able to think anything at anytime, without ever getting any instructions from you. The mind learns from spaced repetition; instructions must become new habits and new behaviours. If you're a one-time or a two-time "Cancel-Cancel" person and stop saying it, the intelligence and independence of a negative subconscious will come back because it doesn't take you seriously. It is VITAL to repeat the command over and over. I'd rather have you say "Cancel-Cancel" all day long than to think about the things or situations you don't want to be thinking about!

Subconscious thoughts are akin to trying to keep a herd of animals together. If you lose one, the rest will follow. In comparison, if one of your negative thoughts is allowed to run off, the rest of your thoughts will follow. "Cancel-Cancel" is like a herding dog keeping all your thoughts together. Once your thoughts are trained to keep everything aligned, it will become simple, easy, and automatic.

It is important to learn to control where you let your thoughts and mind wander. It is vital to your interpretation and quality of life. It is interesting to hear clients discuss how everything is fine as long as they're busy. This usually entails doing something that requires some sort of focus in a certain direction or on a certain task. That is when it's easy to control thoughts. It's when you aren't busy and thoughts come into your head that the trouble starts. This is when you need to realize that your life is yours to live. This is when your choices begin. Your thoughts are your life. When others say, "Your life is up to you," they are right. You must understand and know you can, so that you can and will. What do you do to change things? The first thing is to change your thoughts and your thinking. Change what you focus on. This will change you reality and your belief system.

The Real Secret to Life: Your Thought Processes

There has been much talk about what is "The SECRET to Life?" There is only one secret: the power of your thoughts and your thinking. When you learn to change your thoughts and your thinking, you have now taken control of your life. You are becoming the captain of the ship. Everything now changes. Exciting stuff. It is more exhilarating if you take advantage of this information. The power of your mind. Why are thoughts so vital? They are the beginning of creation. Yes, you can only take action after your thoughts have been created, but only if you want to. Not everyone is looking to be this super-achieving, metropolis building guru. Some people only want peace of mind, calmness and a sense of peacefulness. A time that allows them to be grateful and to appreciate what they already have. They want some relaxation in their lives, or to sleep better and stop the worry. They have achieved a family and perhaps children, and want to be able to enjoy them and themselves. Many of these people, and you are one of them, have already had achievements; perhaps you want many more, maybe a few more, or just to enjoy what you have already. It is up to you and it is all possible.

I see many "unhappy" achievers in my office all the time. Don't confuse achievement and action with happiness. They are NOT the same. Some people will get you to think it is.

Well, sorry to say, it's not. Just because a person is busy doing and achieving things doesn't mean they have peace of mind during times of silence.

I once worked with a very successful business owner with multiple international locations that he travelled to in his private plane. Nonetheless, even with all his financial success and accomplishments, he had one troubling little issue: he couldn't sleep. In times of silence, in other words his time alone, there was no peace. So, was he really in control of his life? It depends on your definition of success.

We can all have success beyond our wildest dreams by creating an inner silence that will calm all storms, ease all difficulties, and create an attitude of optimism and peacefulness. This will give you the success to appreciate all you have, the difficulties that have brought you here, and the confidence to change. Success in any other way is only a façade that people hide behind.

Thought Shifting is about the empowerment of your mind by controlling your thoughts and thinking. You need to understand that it's only through your thoughts and thinking that there can be true empowerment. The elimination of negativity begins by realizing it's there and that there's a choice to accept or reject it. The choice is now to "Cancel-Cancel" it out and to refocus on what you really want, if you could have everything turn out as you desire. Thought Shifting is a simple process that allows you to quickly create change in how you think and how you feel.

Changing Today By Your Thoughts of Tomorrow

It is how you think about the future that determines how you feel today. This is what actually determines how you feel RIGHT NOW. Think about this for a moment: A big push has been to get into the "Now" and to experience life "in the moment." This is a great theory and is about as useful as being told to be positive without being advised how. Who doesn't want to "wake up" and experience the now? The issue is how we perceive the future and **THAT** will determine if we can be in the moment. If you think something bad is going to happen in the future, can you relax right now? Of course not.

Let's look at any issue that is presently a concern for you. If you knew it would never bother you again, would it be an issue right now? NO! If you knew things that are currently bothering you would never ever be an issue in your life, would you still be focusing on them? It is the negativity of one's untrained mind that creates this future of fear and uncertainty, and THAT takes us away from the moment. We aren't supposed to be relaxed and sitting around doing nothing if we think there's danger lurking in front of us. This is hardwired into us for survival. The prime directive of the subconscious is to preserve the body and your life! Remember, perceived fear is real fear. If you imagine anything, you give it the energy and the seed of creation.

How calm can a person be if the negativity in their untrained mind has created future situations that are fearful and dangerous? How can a person enjoy the "NOW" if there is so much worry about their perceived future? But remember, the future can only be imagined, since you haven't been there yet. All worry is negativity. You aren't worried that things will work out perfectly. You aren't afraid that you'll be happy and all your loved ones will be great. You can only worry if your thoughts are on things messing up and not working out as you'd like them to. Now that is pure negative imagination!

In order to be in the "NOW" we must learn how to use our minds in a positive way (which is what you want anyway!) to project what it is that you really desire into the future. The negativity of not being able to be positive has compounded itself into a double dilemma! This is why Thought Shifting is important in creating a future and a "NOW" that'll enhance your life by giving you the life you richly deserve.

An untrained mind will have absorbed the negative environment that now exists in the form of media and fear motivation. Only you can stop this. It's a simple technique that works quickly when you know how.

Thought Sifting is about taking back the power many have surrendered before there was a choice. From an early time, many are submerged in an environment of negativity, worry, and fears. The real truth is not that we should be afraid of the unknown, it is what we know. Someone once taught you how to think the way you do. It's time to regain and reclaim the power of your mind, the power of your thoughts.

Thought Shifting is a decision to be free. It is a choice to create the future that you desire, independent of all thoughts that are not your own. Empowerment is really a freedom to choose those thoughts and to allow you to create your future through the power of your thoughts and thinking. You can be empowered to be in the moment of "NOW" because you're confident in the future. A future that you have created yourself, through the ownership of your thoughts and the power of your imagination. Thought Shifting will awaken you to what is being said and created through your thoughts and by the actions of others. Imagine no longer being led by emotions and thoughts that are not yours.

Welcome to the world of Freedom. Yours to create, experience, and enjoy the way you desire. It doesn't matter what happened or didn't happen. It now matters what you will make happen. It starts in your mind. Instead of waiting to see what comes into your mind, you can now be busy creating the life you desire.

Welcome to the world of Thought Shifting.

"I always believed that if emotions could get locked in quickly then they could be released quickly. Discovering and developing Rapid Emotional Release has proven this."
Rick Saruna

Chapter Thirteen

Rapid Emotional Release (RER)

RER is a system to remove an emotional attachment that results in recurring thoughts and feelings in one's mind. It involves a special process that I developed many years ago, as I heard there was a technique that could quickly remove emotional issues. In an attempt to learn this highly guarded process that they told me I was not qualified for! My determined self decided that I too could remove stuck emotional issues in one session. So I used a combination of processes on my many clients, until I was successful in quickly removing some emotion without reliving the issue. Having perfected this process to help thousands of people who came to our clinic when nothing else worked, we have been able to begin sharing it with the world.

The interesting thing is that as time went by and I was able to get more information on the "other" technique, I discovered they in fact could not remove emotional issues in one session. Therefore, it was my belief and expectancy that I could indeed discover a rapid release process that allowed me to do so. If I would have been taught this other method and was told that it took quite some time to remove issues, I would have also believed that. This is how it all started. It continues today to be an amazing way to help people feel much better and very quickly. Still, this in itself is not the goal. To me, the goal is not just removing the issue, it's teaching someone the tools and showing them ways to create a permanent change in thoughts and thinking to take control of their future.

Unfortunately the process of Rapid Emotional Release and Empowerment cannot be explained on a few pages. It will have to take form in the way of a another book.

Happiness – A One - Two Process

When a client comes to see me, it is not uncommon for them to feel isolated and alone, believing their problem is something no one will understand. They often wonder how weird or strange their issue is, or if it simply exists within their mind. They may even question if the problem is justified or real. I tell them right away, "If you think it and feel it, then it's real." That's because reality only exists inside your head. Everything is based on your points of reference. Things mean what they mean because of what you've experienced and been told; thereby, creating your belief system and sense of reality. Your reality IS your thinking and your thoughts, which becomes your beliefs.

A few years back, a biology professor made a startling discovery most medical doctors might disagree with, as it

Thought Shifting "How To Remove The Negative Inner Voice in 30 Days"

doesn't follow the same thought process that goes with general medical school thinking. This PhD professor and researcher was able to show and demonstrate how a person's belief system actually affected and changed their molecular structure. He writes about changing beliefs and how this has the ability to alter your life. He recommends changing the belief system to transform limitations. One little problem was that he never explained how to actually do it! His discoveries are fascinating, powerful, and life changing. Yet, like everyone else I have seen, read, and listened to over the last 20+ years, he doesn't know a way to show you how to change those limiting beliefs. There are suggestions of using a method to locate the root cause of an issue and to release the emotional attachment that locks it into the past. Except, they aren't nearly as fast and thorough as the Rapid Emotional Release (RER) technique I have developed and use daily in the clinic. The professor's methods only work with past issues and don't do anything for processing your current thinking. When you change old points of reference, of course you'll see things differently. However, there's never been anything available to consciously and constantly allow you to become aware of all thoughts and thinking, then to instantly be able to change them. Removing the past without preparing for the future is like putting out the fire without catching the arsonist. There'll be more problems to put out, because more issues are being created through negative thought processes and everyday thinking. This has always been the issue.

Until now.

The best way to create this change in thinking? The method is with a unique system I developed called Thought Shifting. This technique is what we've covered in earlier chapters to change thought processes: through the words we say; being aware of our environment; and also to control our inner thought processes, with our specialized keyword technique to work on the inner voice.

Removing Locked-In Negative Emotions

Rapid Emotional Release (RER) removes trauma and other issues locked in as emotional references, which are a person's reality. It's their dictionary of life and their encyclopedia of life's meanings. It's from here all references are made and interpreted from thoughts into meanings. Emotions are what make an experience meaningful. If there were no emotions, life would lack meaning and excitement. Emotions keep us safe, by locking in a memory and reminding us not to repeat certain behaviours that hurt or let us know it's safe to repeat pleasurable things.

This is the process and the meaning behind all emotions. It's meant to preserve life and increase the quality of living. Unfortunately, negative emotions and events are locked in the subconscious the same way as positive ones. If we look at your personal history, all your experiences and "connect the dots," you'll be able to understand why you feel the way you do. Everything is connected. One thought leads to another, then another, until you're way over there on some tangent, usually a place you didn't intend or want to be! It is okay; you simply allowed your thoughts to literally float away. Yes, you allowed them. It might feel like you had no choice, but you did and still do.

A client came to me all stressed out, feeling like no one could ever relate to what he was going through. I said, "If someone went through the same things you've been through, the same parents, the same teachers, the same negative relatives, the identical experiences, do you know who they'd be? They would be YOU!"

It doesn't take long before thinking takes on a certain pattern or behaviour. All children are born rich. They aren't diamonds in the rough; they are diamonds that we rough up. Most children are NOT born anxious, nervous, or phobic. These problems are learned, and then situations are emotionalized and stored, becoming points of reference (good, bad, or ugly). It really doesn't matter though. What does matter is how we try to make sense of our life, based on what we remember. As knowledge is stored, it's locked into the subconscious. Every memory and thought will refer back to a point of reference. We only know what we know, and how we know it can only be based on the time we first experienced it. All memories are stored like a picture at the time it was taken. A snapshot in-time could describe it. If you took a picture 20 years ago, every time you look at it you only see it how it happened back then. You can only see it through the eyes of who you were when you experienced it. It's really a fascinating process. Yet, this is where most people get into trouble. They attempt to function in today's world with points of reference from the past. All memory is a regression, as we go back to what happened and how we experienced it at a particular time. Unfortunately, you don't go back as you are today, but instead you become that person you were when the incident occurred! So, for us adults, we're actually living in a world filled with references and memories from many years ago. In fact, memories from childhood can make or break a person's current quality of life. It's like going through the motions today, while trying to figure out what happened yesterday. For many, the past is unfinished business, but the newsflash is that it's finished; unfortunately, most people don't like the way things ended. If everything ended in the way you wanted them to, you wouldn't be thinking about it over and over.

I remember working with a man who closed his eyes and began telling me stories about issues that occurred to him when he was 5-years-old. It was captivating listening to these tales filled with such detail and clarity; you'd have guessed they'd taken place earlier that morning. What was even more interesting was this man was 80-years-old! These events being told off the top of his head had happened 75 years ago. I am so impressed when I have clients over the age of 70, who come in looking to change their thinking. It doesn't matter how old you are, it's always NOW and there is never a better time to do anything than right now.

One lady I am particularly proud of came to me with a host of issues, including negative thoughts, and was filled with worry. This type of case is something that I repeatedly see. This woman was so wonderful because as I worked on removing negative issues through my RER process, every week she'd report a positive change in her thoughts and feelings. She no longer had to suffer or be imprisoned by the old thoughts from the past. Then I taught her Thought Shifting, so she could create the thoughts she desired. It really is an amazing process. It's not just about releasing the past, it's about learning to think differently and have new things to look forward to in the future. It's about learning to take the opportunity that every situation gives you to create a future of hope, health, harmony, and the life you desire and deserve.

Whenever I present at conferences or keynotes, I talk about the importance of two things: removing the main emotional issues (usually negative experiences) and then changing thinking. If you don't change thoughts and thinking, you're simply waiting for more negativity because it's all you ever knew and still all you know.

I recently spoke at two major events, teaching Advanced Techniques of the Mind to therapists specializing in hypnosis. I stressed how important it is to get to the root cause of the real issue in order to create lasting change, but there's also a problem with that. Removing something an individual has relied on for so long creates quite the void in their mind. This is why learning to think is vital. If a person doesn't know how to think and create change in their thoughts, they'll simply recreate more difficulties in the future. This is the shortfall of the whole concept of being "in the now." It's very difficult, and actually impossible, to be in the now if your thoughts of the future are negative. The quickest and easiest way to be in the now, full of life and experiencing every moment, is to have confidence that the future will be safe, happy, and healthy. This isn't only the concept of Thought Shifting; it's the key to happiness and living your life free from the past.

The mind is an intriguing and powerful tool. Like any tool, its power or ability is limited to the skill of the user. This is why it's so essential to know how to use and control the power of your mind. The real power lies in your ability to create changes in your thoughts and your thinking.

How Does the Mind Actually Work?

Let's look for a moment at how the mind works. There is the conscious and the subconscious. The conscious mind is analytical and is your willpower. It also works with a concept known as time and space. This is the tip of the iceberg. We are thinking consciously right now. We like to believe that the conscious is in control; although, this is where the misconception begins. In fact, I like to think of it not as the tip of the iceberg, but rather a snowflake on the iceberg. The other part of this massive iceberg is the subconscious. It's not only powerful like the iceberg below the surface, but we don't know its depth nor realize its influence and strength.

Through the years, the subconscious is the area people have been chasing to understand and figure out. It hasn't been easy. There are many theories and explanations about the subconscious and consciousness, but they are just that: theory. Theory is great and it's where all searches seem to begin. It's an attempt to find the answers and solutions. The amazing part is that it's quite simple and easy, as the answer lies within each and every one of us. Yes, YOU have the answer. It is inherently given to you and it lies deep within, yet is it really that deep? Of course that depends on what you think deep is.

The way I look at this question is quite different than most individuals. It has to be different, because the ways most people have been analyzing thinking hasn't been working. The subconscious is really the core concept; although the focus is not necessarily on understanding it, as much as it has to be on changing it. I want you to understand just enough to make the necessary changes in order to transform your life. We will not focus on theory as much as the information that will help you make changes. I want you to have an understanding of how it works and how to make it work. All of this has been proven in my day-to-day experiences, not out of textbooks, but through years of working with people from all walks of life. It's through their experiences I've been able to take some simple processes and apply them to everyone's lives.

There are still choices and options to consider on the road to happiness. Undirected thinking can often complicate and compound itself, just like the issues in a person's life. For example, as an issue appears, it creates a problem and then that problem in itself becomes greater than the issue that actually created it. A person can be upset about someone or something and not want to repeat that situation, causing anxiety to develop. Then the anxiety becomes the issue and the focus changes from the original problem to the reaction in the body. Now you need to eliminate the anxiety. You would think the best way to get rid of the issue would be to look at the issue or the initial cause. You would think that, wouldn't you? Well, that's always been my belief and the way I teach my clients.

"Always look for the root cause and initial issues, no matter how long ago they occurred, as this is the way the subconscious works. Remember, I don't write the rules; I only interpret them and make them work for you.

RER – Rapid Emotional Release is a special process that removes stuck emotional issues. The process has been proven on thousands of people who receive very rapid results in most cases. I say most cases, because there are many variables involved in getting someone back to health and well-being.

I developed Thought Shifting in the 1990's and discovered and designed RER in 2000.The combination of the two was quickly put together, freeing people from their emotional difficulties and teaching them to live a life free from the past.

The nicest thing about RER is that it works on any STUCK emotional issue. If it's a recurring thought or feeling, once it's released, it loses its power because the only thing that was keeping it there was an emotion. In other words, the thought is "emotionalized" and without the emotion, there's no reaction in the body; therefore, it doesn't stay in the mind. This whole concept might be difficult for many to comprehend, as it's different than any other type of psychological process.

RER is available in our office where we use it daily with our clients. We are also beginning to train other therapists in these techniques and methods. The process is non-invasive and you don't have to talk about or retell all the emotional details like conventional therapy. The therapist will be using Thought Shifting dialogue in combination with an "eyes open" process of specific eye patterns (which are very unique and can vary amongst people in how they are applied).

Most people report an instant change in feelings and thoughts. The body becomes more relaxed and the emotion dissolves for that particular issue. Then we move on to the next layer. It's very possible to create some huge changes in one session. Certain problems may take several sessions to find the "real issues," if they're hidden or the client says they don't know why or how they feel this way.

Remember it's not just removing the emotion, it's learning to think and process differently. Removing the emotion is an amazing sense of relief, but learning to think differently with Thought Shifting will change your life forever.

"Chaos always comes before opportunity. It wakes you up and makes you pay attention. It provides that moment of awareness that allows you to change everything."
Rick Saruna

Chapter Fourteen

When Looking For Help

The days of not asking for help are almost gone. I say almost, because many people are still reluctant to seek advice about traumatic issues that haunt them like a bad dream or a one channel TV rerun. I see more and more clients looking for relief. It wasn't always this way. Issues of the mind, be them mood or emotion, were usually not discussed and left to accumulate, finally erupting into serious health issues, both physically and mentally. Issues hidden under labels like "depression" and "insomnia" don't go away on their own, the same way they don't develop on their own.

Acknowledging there's an issue may be difficult to do. If this is the case, instead, why not just admit you know things can be better? No one will perceive that negatively because you're actually looking at it in a positive way.

Remember, you don't need to have a problem to want to feel better, maximize your potential, or get more out of life. I've worked with very successful people who had serious issues that I promise you wouldn't want to experience. We're all different, yet also all the same. So let's find our similarities in order to learn what works and apply it into our lives. It doesn't matter where you are in life or where you think you should be. It can all be changed and greatly improved to levels you may never have allowed yourself to imagine. When you change your thoughts, you change your thinking, your emotional responses change, and then your life changes forever.

Let's maximize whatever you're doing or always wanted to do. Personal and business issues (struggles or situations) and peak performance (individual or teams) can be improved through the processes we do, starting with the material in this book. Use it, apply it, and continually seek improvement through happiness and health.

Your Mission? To Create Change

Many of you have been on a mission to create change, working with others in an attempt to live a fuller and more meaningful life. No doubt some have found success while others have not, which isn't surprising. Don't feel alone or believe that there's nothing that can be done, as this is just not true. Maybe you've been to therapists, doctors, specialists, and the like, which is fabulous because this is where change begins. However, it still might not be the answer you desire. There are various reasons for this. It might be that the person you sought help from practices a style of therapy that focuses on the past, rather than the future. It could be the therapist or maybe you were not ready for change. I find it interesting that people don't think twice about spending $100going out to a bar, restaurant, concert, or sporting event, but hesitate to change their lives from the inside out for financial reasons.

The most important thing to remember is all therapists are not the same, just as all doctors are different from one another. If a person goes for counselling and doesn't get the results they hoped for, it doesn't mean counselling won't or doesn't work. There are many varieties of therapy styles. As we develop, grow, and gain experience, we change and we are not the same. The whole process is how we evolve. Our experiences, lessons, acquired knowledge, and wisdom come as we mature. The same is true of medical care and treatments. There's a difference in who is providing care, their abilities and attitudes, with their own beliefs. Never let someone hold you back based on their limiting viewpoints. No one knows ALL of the latest and up-to-date methods and techniques.

People have always doubted or ridiculed new ideas and inventions. Let yourself be that next new invention by reinventing yourself, your thoughts, your thinking, and your health. If it's possible, then it's possible for you to be the exception to the rule and beat the odds, starting today. I want to learn and take lessons from people like you, who've decided to defy the status quo and brave a new path. Those are the people we all need to spend more time with; learning the attitudes and beliefs they used to get better, even when others doubted it was possible. You don't have to accept an opinion that's against your better judgment and desires. I challenge you to be the one who beats the odds!

In most cases of health, when one has hope, your immunity will be higher and your recovery will be quicker.

Those with no hope, who buy into someone else's belief that there are no options for change, quickly become what others believe they should be. This negative thinking might be unhealthy advice causing permanent damage without any possibility of improvement, even though medical advances are changing at an unprecedented rate. It's a proven fact that many people improve in direct relation to the attitude of their attending health professional. Pick someone that believes in you, more than you believe in yourself.

I love the internet, the information highway. Like any highway, there are two sides or directions you can take. You have the right direction and the wrong direction. There's a right side and the wrong side. It's up to you to determine which side you want to be on and what information you want to surround yourself with on a daily basis. I've had many clients become distraught by researching the internet, which is unfortunate. On the other hand, I know people who've become empowered by it, reading stories about individuals who've accomplished feats they never thought possible until realizing, "If others can do it, so can I!" This is exactly what my belief is as well. I believe in the possibility that you can be as much or as little that you decide you'd like to be. You will accomplish and achieve what you let yourself believe you can.

In my clinic, this has always been my mindset when working with people or when talking to a group. It is all possible. Someone has to be first, someone has to defy odds, and someone has to lead the way.

I ask, "Why not you?"

Pay attention to yourself before anyone else. Observe, listen, and learn, but always remember the highway. Stay on the side that'll take you where you want to go and where you want to end up. There will be detours, roadblocks, and diversions. So what! Keep what's important close at heart and never let anyone talk you into a limiting belief. This is not a game or dress rehearsal, it's your life. Live it and experience it. When life is easy and things flow, everything is simple. It's when things don't quite go your way that you need to focus on simplifying your life, to make sure you'll continue on the path you've chosen.

I find many of the troubles in most people's lives are really issues they've created and empowered in their minds. If problems can be created, then so can the solutions. The purpose of this book is to make people aware of how easy things really can and should be.

It is important to surround yourself with many people who also believe in the possibility of possibilities - this thing called hope. When you have those individuals, hang onto them, and appreciate them as much as they'll also appreciate you.

Live, love, laugh, and above all cherish this wonderful opportunity we've been given called Life. Experience all it has to offer and all that you have to offer the world. Create the change and be the progress. You not only earned it, you deserve it.

Contacting Me – Rick Saruna

I have many answers and solutions and I welcome you to contact my office. You may be in a position to come see me directly, which would be fantastic. I have had many people arrive at the clinic and spend days creating changes to the many issues they never thought would change. I am able to help through phone sessions as well, offering answers, solutions, and consultations. I also can teach and present these processes of Thought Shifting and Rapid Emotional Release to individuals or groups. We have a variety of online programs and resources too. Contact our office and website. I am available for conferences and presentations for corporations and special situations. In addition, I can help a sports team or corporate team with thought changes, negativity removal, positive empowerment, or simply get anyone out of any slump.

We can be reached at our head office.

Body & Mind Natural Health,
2303 Central Ave.,
Windsor, Ontario,
N8W4J1.
Office (519) 948-0078
www.StressFree.net

Manufactured by Amazon.ca
Bolton, ON